# Sounds Like Fun!

rite the missing words. Use words from the box.

| | | |
|---|---|---|
| nephew | coughed | orphanage |
| rough | alphabet | enough |
| autograph | laugh | graph |
| paragraph | trough | gopher |
| telephone | pheasant | photo |

1. Take a ____________________ with a camera.
2. I wrote a ____________________ about my trip.
3. I talked to Grandma on the ____________________ .
4. How many letters are in the ____________________ ?
5. Jokes make me ____________________ .
6. Let's make a bar ____________________ .
7. I've had ____________________ cereal, thank you.
8. She wrote her ____________________ in my book!
9. Stanley ____________________ and sneezed all night.
10. The water was too ____________________ to go water skiing.
11. The farmer filled the pig's ____________________ with garbage.
12. The ____________________ was digging up all of the flowers.
13. My ____________________ came to visit over spring break.
14. Manuel lived at the ____________________ until he was three.
15. The ____________________ escaped from the hunters.

# Get Out of Our House!

In some words one vowel sound blends with another vowel sound to make a combined sound, as *ou* in *house*, or *ow* in *cow*. The *ou* and *ow* make the same sound.

Write the missing words. Use words from the box.

| | | |
|---|---|---|
| sound | growl | howl |
| flower | around | cloud |
| crowd | ounces | town |
| down | found | outside |
| loudly | bounced | |

1. A bee buzzes near a ____________________ .

2. See the fluffy ____________________ in the sky.
3. It was sunny and warm ____________________ .
4. Coyotes ____________________ at night.
5. Did you hear that ____________________ ?
6. The circus came to ____________________ .
7. The man skied ____________________ the hill too quickly.
8. A large ____________________ of people went inside the tent.
9. Dad bought nine ____________________ of juice.
10. Bears ____________________ when they're hungry.
11. You must run ____________________ the track twice.
12. Edan ____________________ a watch.
13. A lion roars ____________________ .
14. A little girl ____________________ a ball on the sidewalk.

# Fact or Opinion?

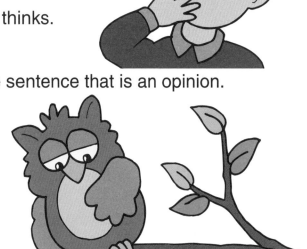

**fact** is something that has happened or is real.

Example: We breathe air.

n **opinion** is something someone believes or thinks.

Example: I think the air smells funny.

nderline the sentence that is a fact. Circle the sentence that is an opinion.

. An owl is a kind of bird.

Owls are the wisest birds.

2. Reptiles do not make good pets.

Some animals are reptiles.

3. People can buy bread at a store.

Homemade bread is much tastier than bread from a store.

4. Fried chicken makes a delicious meal.

Chicken is a type of meat.

5. A pen pal is a person who writes letters.

I think it is fun to receive letters.

6. Books are more fun than television.

Some books tell about real people.

7. I think spiders are ugly.

A spider is an animal with eight legs.

# That's a Fact!

A **fact** is something that can be proven.

Example: Many people keep dogs or cats as pets.

An **opinion** expresses someone's feelings about a person, thing, or an idea.

Example: Dogs are better pets than cats.

Read each sentence. Write whether it is a *fact* or an *opinion*.

| | | | |
|---|---|---|---|
| 1. A bear is an animal. ____________ | 2. Wood comes from trees. ____________ | 3. I think trucks are better than cars. ____________ | 4. Robins are prettier than blue jays. ____________ |
| 5. Some birds fly south for the winter. ____________ | 6. A clock is used to tell time. ____________ | 7. Hats look silly. ____________ | 8. Country music is great. ____________ |
| 9. Pizza is delicious. ____________ | 10. I think dresses are pretty. ____________ | 11. A whale is a mammal. ____________ | 12. Hamsters have fur. ____________ |

# What Will Happen Next?

ften clues in a story will help you predict what will happen next. For example, if the ıaracters are putting on raincoats and talking about dark, heavy-looking clouds, you ın guess it might rain in the story.

ead the following paragraphs.
ill in the circle that best predicts what will happen next.

---

. "Let's clean up," said Mrs. Perez. "It's nearly time to go home." Andre hurried to the pet corner to take care of the hamster. Just as he was fastening the door to the hamster cage, the fire alarm rang. The teacher and children quickly left the building. The hamster looked at the half-closed door and then

◯ closed the door. ◯ escaped. ◯ went to sleep.

---

2. Ashley passed a pet store on the way home from school. In the window, she saw a cute puppy. Ashley put her hand on the window near the puppy. It jumped at her hand and licked the window, wagging its tail. Ashley

◯ went in to see the pup. ◯ ran away in fright. ◯ drove a car.

---

3. April took her dog, Tasha, for a walk on the beach. What a beautiful day! There were many people out walking their dogs. Suddenly a black cat stepped out from behind a rock. Tasha

◯ entered a race. ◯ got on a train. ◯ chased the cat.

---

# You Decide

Often clues in a story help you predict what will happen next. Many times a story could end in several ways.

Read each of the following paragraphs. Write an ending to each story.

1. The wild horses grazed peacefully in the meadow. Robin and her mother hid in the tall grass, watching. "That's the one I want," Robin said hopefully. "I like the little filly with brown and white spots." What happened next?

______________________________

______________________________

______________________________

______________________________

2. Jake and his family had just moved into their new house. One day as he looked out the front window, Jake saw two boys about his age on bicycles. He wished he knew them and could go out and play. Just then, Jake's father came in from the garage. "Jake, we just unpacked your bike," his father said. What happened next?

______________________________

______________________________

______________________________

______________________________

# In Order

umber the sentences 1, 2, 3, and 4 to show the order.

____ Caitlin waved the flower and the bug flew away.

____ A red bug walked on Caitlin's flower.

____ The bug had tiny black dots on its back.

____ Caitlin picked a flower.

____ It started to rain.

____ We watched as the drops fell against the window.

____ We went out to play in the mud puddles.

____ Then the sun came out.

____ Jon went outside.

____ The alarm clock rang.

____ Jon slept with his puppy.

____ He got up and got dressed.

____ Then she walked to the pool and jumped in the water.

____ After her mother said yes, Rosa put on her swimsuit.

____ She asked her mother if she could go to the pool.

____ Rosa wanted to go swimming.

# Dressing for a Play

Pretend you are a clown and are getting dressed for your part in a play. Read each sentence below. Write the sentences in order and draw a picture of each sentence.

Finally, put on a red nose and an orange fuzzy wig and go on stage.
First, get into your blue and red clown costume.
Next, put a makeup cape over your costume.
Make up your face.
Then take off the makeup cape.

| 1. | 2. | 3. | 4. | 5. |
|---|---|---|---|---|
| | | | | |

# Word Detective

ometimes when you read, you see an unfamiliar ord. To find out what that word means, you can use l of the words near it as clues.

se the word clues in the sentences below to help entify the meaning of each **purple** word.

. The artist created a **sculpture** out of clay. The **sculpture** was shaped like a giraffe.

A sculpture is

◯ a costume ◯ a poster ◯ a statue

. The people enjoyed the **concert**. The music at the **concert** was played by a band.

A concert is

◯ a large building ◯ a kind of food ◯ a musical performance

3. When riding on the train, some **passengers** talked quietly while others read books.

A passenger is a

◯ talker ◯ rider ◯ reader

4. The **boulder** rolled down the hill and blocked the road.

A boulder is

◯ a large rock ◯ a person ◯ a small rock

5. We had to **interview** a friend. I asked her 20 questions in the **interview**.

An interview is

◯ a meeting with someone to get information

◯ information you would find in a dictionary

◯ a party

# Which Bat Is That?

Many words have more than one meaning. You can find the meaning of these words by looking at the other words in the sentence.

Read the sentences. Use the word clues to help you find the meaning of the **green** word. Circle the meaning of the **green** word.

1. The screeching **bat** flew into the cave.

   an animal — a stick used to hit a ball — to blink; wink; flutter

2. The baby cried when she dropped her **rattle**.

   a noise — a toy — a snake's tail

3. A storekeeper gave Sam **change** from a dollar.

   money left over — make something different — to trade

4. The driver **steers** the car around the corner.

   beef cattle — guides in a certain way — a tip

5. The **duck** flew south for the winter.

   a kind of bird — lower your head or body — a kind of cloth

6. Will you **hand** that magazine to me?

   a part of the body — pass — near

# Making New Words

prefix is a group of letters added to the beginning of a base ord. A prefix changes the meaning of the word. Here are me common prefixes.

| Prefix | Meaning |
|---|---|
| dis | the opposite of |
| un | the opposite of; not |
| re | again |
| de | away from; off |

ead each word in the word box. Add *dis* or *un* to each word. hen complete each sentence below with the new word.

**Word Box**

______ even ______ order ______ obey ______ plug

. You won't find the pen with your desk in such ________________.

. Jake does not ________________ his mother.

. Don't trip. The sidewalk is ________________.

. Be sure to ________________ the toaster before you clean it.

ircle the word that best completes each sentence.

. Put out the campfire. It's time to ________________ and leave.

rebuild decamp repay

. Our flight has landed. Let's ________________ now.

decamp deplane debug

7. The school collapsed in the earthquake. Let's ________________ it.

rebuild repay reelect

# Change That Word!

A **suffix** is a group of letters added to the end of a base word. A suffix changes the meaning of the word. Here are some common suffixes.

| **Suffix** | **Meaning** |
|---|---|
| ous | full of; having |
| ful | full of; causing |
| less | without; lacking |
| able | capable of |

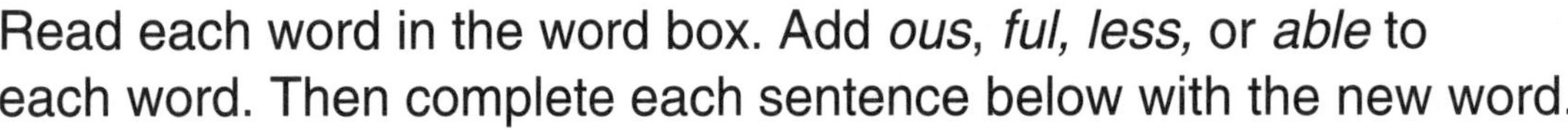

Read each word in the word box. Add *ous*, *ful, less,* or *able* to each word. Then complete each sentence below with the new word.

**Word Box**

marvel_______ breath ______ peace ______ bend_______

1. The new toy racecar tracks are_______________________.
2. Sheila had a __________________time at the birthday party.
3. The______________________music drifted through the halls.
4. The students were___________________ after running around the track.

Add a suffix from the top of the page to each word below. Write the meaning of the new word.

5. courage **ous**     **full of courage**
6. danger__________     ______________________
7. time__________     ______________________
8. treat__________     ______________________
9. wonder __________     ______________________

# Syllable Symphony

rite the number of vowel letters you see in each word.
hen write the number of vowel sounds you hear in each word.

There are as many syllables in a word as there are vowel sounds in the word.

| | Vowel Letters | Vowel Sounds |
|---|---|---|
| conductor | 3 | 3 |
| flute | ____ | ____ |
| trumpet | ____ | ____ |
| trombone | ____ | ____ |
| orchestra | ____ | ____ |
| tuba | ____ | ____ |

Vrite the number of syllables in each word.

7. drums 1
8. music ____
9. concert ____
10. violin ____
11. piano ____
12. harmony ____
13. cymbals ____
14. guitar ____

# Parts Apart

When the first vowel in a word is followed by two consonants, the word is usually divided into syllables between the two consonants.

Example: mag net    rib bon

Write the word in syllables.

1. ladder **lad der**
2. compound ________
3. orbit ________
4. hammer ________
5. publish ________
6. enter ________
7. arrow ________
8. center ________
9. gallop ________
10. mustard ________

Write the number of syllables in each word.

11. hiking **2**
12. squirrel ____
13. sunflower ____
14. supervisor ____
15. together ____
16. whispering ____
17. suddenly ____
18. riverbank ____

# What's the Idea?

The **main idea** is what the paragraph is about.
**Supporting details** help prove the main idea.

n each paragraph below, circle the main idea and underline the supporting details.

1. Hiking in springtime can be interesting. Last May, I saw a mother bear and her three playful cubs across the river. I also saw a doe with her white-spotted fawn.

2. My dog greets me when I come home from school. We share snacks and sleep together in my bed. If I feel lonely, I can talk to my dog and she always listens. It's nice to have a pet.

3. Deserts are full of life. At first glance, it may seem as if nothing lives there. If you look closely, though, you will see animal tracks in the sand. Under rocks and in holes live small animals, insects, and reptiles.

4. Texas is an interesting place. It can take several days to drive across Texas. As you drive, you see many things. On the plains, cowboys round up cattle and drills bring up oil.

# The Main Idea

Every paragraph has a main idea.
The other sentences give details that explain the main idea.

Read each main idea below and the sentences that follow it.
Fill in the circle next to each sentence that supports the main idea.

1. Penguins are unusual birds.
   - ◯ Penguins stand upright on very short legs.
   - ◯ Penguins walk with an amusing, clumsy waddle.
   - ◯ Their scale-like feathers help keep them warm.

2. Emperor penguin fathers hatch and care for chicks.
   - ◯ Killer whales like to eat penguins.
   - ◯ Each dad holds an egg on his feet until it hatches.
   - ◯ His feathers and skin help keep the egg warm.

3. Penguins have wings but do not fly.
   - ◯ Their wings are small and have no flight feathers.
   - ◯ These birds use their wings to swim.
   - ◯ The water is really cold.

4. Some penguins have funny names.
   - ◯ The female returns after two months of swimming.
   - ◯ Macaroni penguins have strange head feathers.
   - ◯ Little blue penguins come from Australia.

5. Penguins have different habits than other birds.
   - ◯ Penguins spend much of their lives in the water.
   - ◯ Penguins are excellent swimmers.
   - ◯ On land, they build enormous nests called rookeries.

# What Happened?

ne event may cause another to happen. For example, ourtney falling off her bike may cause her to scrape her knee.

rite a sentence from the box to finish each cause or effect.

| ause | Effect |
|---|---|
| ________________________ | The dog barked. |
| . Beth splashed water on Ron. | ________________________ |
| . ________________________ | Laurie squealed. |
| . The smoke rose to the ceiling. | ________________________ |
| . ________________________ | The room got dark. |
| . We left food on the picnic table. | ________________________ |

**Sentence Box**

| | |
|---|---|
| The candle burned out. | He got wet. |
| A stranger knocked on the door. | The ants ate the food. |
| Adam crept up and tapped her arm. | The fire alarm sounded. |

# Which Is Which?

An **effect** is what happens.
A **cause** is the reason something happens.

Example: I went outside because my friends called to me.
Effect—I went outside.
Cause—My friends called to me.

Read each of the following sentences. Then answer the questions on the lines provided. Write in complete sentences.

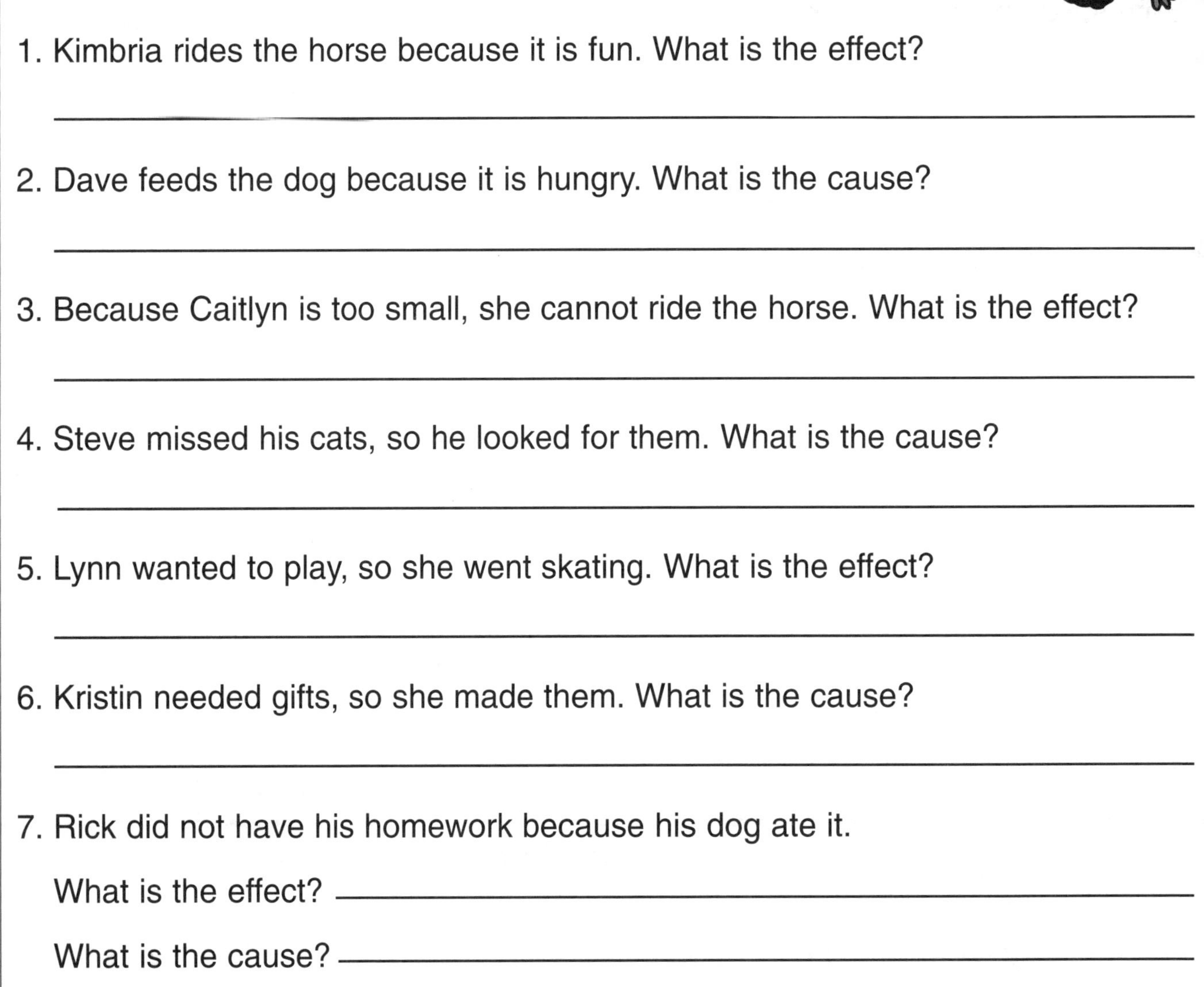

1. Kimbria rides the horse because it is fun. What is the effect?

______________________________

2. Dave feeds the dog because it is hungry. What is the cause?

______________________________

3. Because Caitlyn is too small, she cannot ride the horse. What is the effect?

______________________________

4. Steve missed his cats, so he looked for them. What is the cause?

______________________________

5. Lynn wanted to play, so she went skating. What is the effect?

______________________________

6. Kristin needed gifts, so she made them. What is the cause?

______________________________

7. Rick did not have his homework because his dog ate it.

What is the effect? ______________________________

What is the cause? ______________________________

# Soaring With Synonyms

**Synonyms** are words that have the same or almost the same meaning. Choose a synonym from the hot-air balloon to replace the **blue** word in each sentence.

| | |
|---|---|
| ate | leave |
| helped | walked |
| kind | happy |
| journey | angry |
| argued | hid |

1. The airplane will **depart** at six o'clock.

   ______________________________

2. The bear **devoured** our picnic.

   ______________________________

3. Mia was **ecstatic** when she won the race.

   ______________________________

4. Chico **concealed** the dog under his bed.

   ______________________________

5. Mom was **furious** when I broke her vase.

   ______________________________

6. The **thoughtful** man invited everyone to the party.

   ______________________________

7. Hannah and Elsa **strolled** through the park.

   ______________________________

8. We had a pleasant **voyage** on an ocean liner.

   ______________________________

9. Roberto **assisted** Veronica in carrying the books to the library.

   ______________________________

10. The boy **quarreled** with his mother about doing his homework.

   ______________________________

# It's the Opposite

**Antonyms** are words that have opposite meanings.
Choose the correct word to complete each sentence.

**enormous** **tiny**

1. An ______________________ elephant trampled through the jungle
2. The ______________________ mouse scurried into the hole.

**tense** **relaxed**

3. Sonja was very nervous and ______________________ before her speech.
4. My father is ______________________ after he exercises.

**awkward** **graceful**

5. Ethan looked very ______________________ when he first began rollerblading.
6. The Olympic ice skaters are extremely ______________________ when they are skating.

**eager** **reluctant**

7. Udi was ______________________ to take the test that he had been studying for.
8. Dave was ______________________ to dive off the diving board because he was afraid of heights.

# Person, Place, or Thing?

**common noun** names any person, place, or thing.

Example: girl

**proper noun** names a special person, place, or thing.

Example: Joyce

ook at the nouns in the bag of gumballs.
rite each noun in the correct gumball machine.

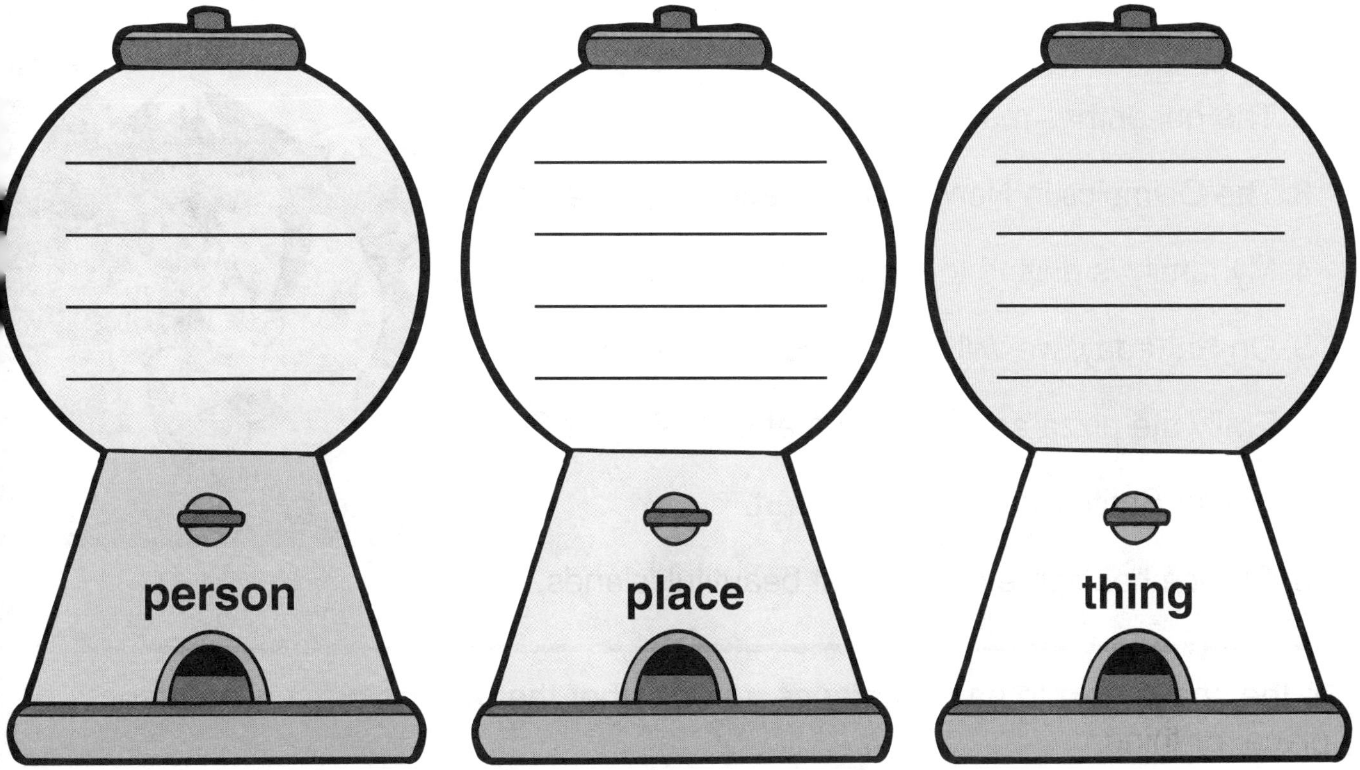

**person** ____________________ ____________________ ____________________ ____________________

**place** ____________________ ____________________ ____________________ ____________________

**thing** ____________________ ____________________ ____________________ ____________________

Circle the common nouns and underline the proper nouns.

1. Linda, come here.
2. Draw the picture, please.
3. Grandma is sleeping.
4. Patterson School is fun.
5. The clock ticked.
6. LaNell is happy.
7. Max laughed.
8. Did you find your book?
9. Balls bounce.
10. Buy that car.
11. Mice play.
12. Hit the net!

# More Nouns

A **common noun** is the name of a person, place, or thing.

Example: mountains

A **proper noun** is the name of a special person, place, or thing.

Example: Canada

In each sentence below, underline the common nouns once and the proper nouns twice.

1. Italy is a beautiful country with famous buildings.
2. The queen has many little dogs.
3. The Olympics in Norway and France were beautiful.
4. My family is driving to the Grand Canyon for vacation.
5. On Saturday, we will have a picnic at Wildwood Park.
6. Emily ate pizza and ice cream at Little Flower School.
7. Doctor Smith listened to my heart.
8. Greece has some of the most beautiful islands.

In the space next to each sentence, tell whether the **orange** noun is a person, place, or thing.

9. The Gobi is a huge **desert** in Mongolia. ______________________
10. A koala is a small animal from **Australia**. ______________________
11. **Birgitt** was born in Germany. ______________________
12. Visitors to New York can see the **Statue of Liberty**. ______________________
13. **Guam** is an island in the Pacific Ocean. ______________________
14. The **sea horse** looks very different from most fish. ______________________

# Spring Subjects

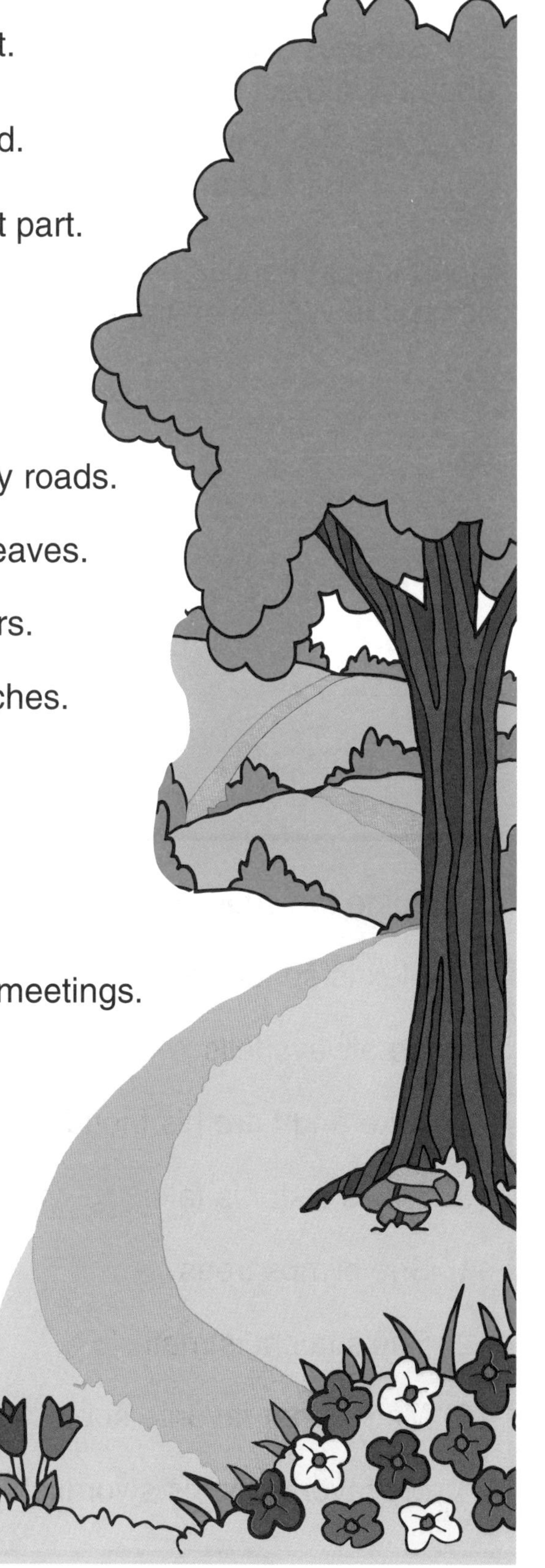

ıe **subject** is what or whom the sentence is about.
subject can be one word or more than one word.

Examples: **Karla and Kim** went to Disneyland.
**Disneyland** was a lot of fun.
**The roller coasters** were the best part.

ɪnderline the subject in each sentence.

1. We are glad spring came early this year.
2. The wildflowers are blooming along the country roads.
3. All the trees in my neighborhood have green leaves.
4. My favorite tree is a dogwood with white flowers.
5. I love to climb great big trees with lots of branches.
6. One of my friends has a secret tree house.
7. Our neighborhood club is called the Eagles.
8. We hold a meeting every Saturday in summer.
9. Mom and Dad are not allowed to come to our meetings.
10. They must be curious about what we do!
11. Mom and I planted a lot of tulip bulbs last fall.
12. The bulbs have now grown into flowers.
13. I especially like the red and yellow tulips.
14. My friends and I play baseball in the spring.
15. Jill is the best pitcher in our league.
16. I hope to hit a home run this season.

# Name That Subject!

The **subject** of a sentence tells what or whom the sentence is about. A subject can be one word or more than one word.

Example: **Purple** is Laura's favorite color.
**Laura's dress** is blue and purple.

Read the sentences below. Provide a subject of your own for each sentence. Write it on the line.

1. ______________________________ is my favorite color.
2. ______________________________ is my best friend.
3. ______________________________ tastes terrific.
4. __________________________ is my favorite sandwich.
5. __________________________ makes me so happy!
6. A ______________________ is the pet of my dreams.

Underline the subject of each of the following sentences.

7. Alex is so funny!
8. He always tells jokes.
9. Jake and I are his friends.
10. Alex's sister is talented, too.
11. She climbs trees.
12. Sue's talent is math.
13. Math is her favorite subject.
14. My favorite fish is swordfish.
15. Tom and Kim like to play soccer.
16. The two men laughed at the clown.
17. My neighbors enjoy working in the yard.
18. The library closes at six o'clock.
19. The milk was sour!
20. The computer broke down.
21. Penguins are fun to watch.
22. Steve and Jeremy rode their bikes.

# What Is a Predicate?

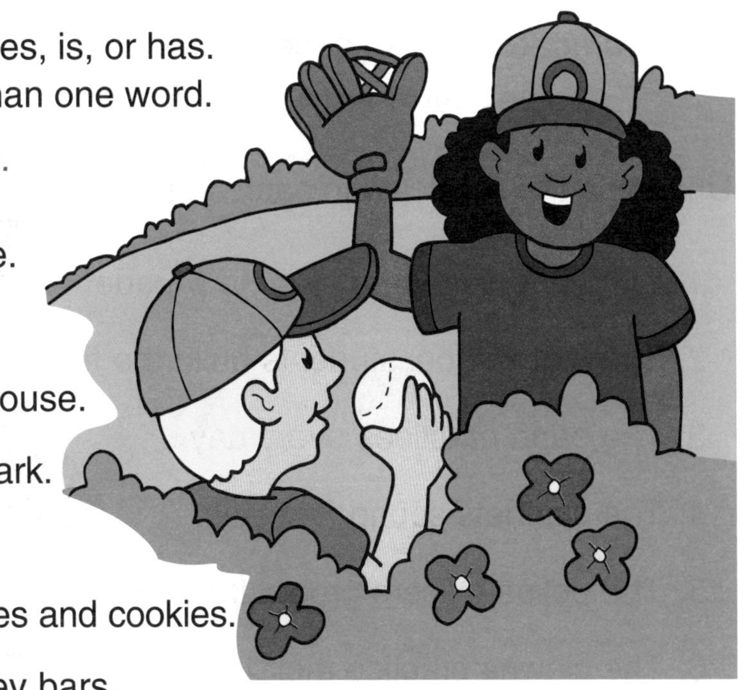

ıe **predicate** tells what the subject does, is, or has. predicate can be one word or more than one word.

Example: Morgan **likes squirrels**.

Circle the predicate in each sentence.

1. Michael packed a picnic lunch.
2. He rode his bike to his friend's house.
3. Kay and Michael walked to the park.
4. They played baseball.
5. They ate peanut butter sandwiches and cookies.
6. Then they climbed on the monkey bars.

Each sentence is missing a predicate. Write a predicate from the phrase box to complete each sentence.

| Phrase Box | |
|---|---|
| live in Calgary, Canada | build nests in springtime |
| sells ice cream | performs tricks with a rabbit |
| is gray today | got a new bike for my birthday |

7. My friends ______
8. Birds ______
9. Max the magician ______
10. I ______
11. The sky ______
12. The ice-cream vendor ______

# Predicate Parade

The **predicate** of a sentence tells what action the subject does.

Example: David **ate a huge hot dog**.

Underline the predicate in each sentence.

1. Everyone gets ready for the parade.
2. The high school students build the floats.
3. The band practices every day.
4. The clarinets sound fantastic.
5. The police officers groom their horses.
6. The clowns practice their tricks.
7. People hang up flags.
8. People line up along the sidewalks.
9. The parade goes down Main Street.
10. The tuba players sway back and forth to the beat.
11. The band members wear tall hats.
12. The twirlers throw and catch their batons.
13. The clowns pass out candy.
14. Some men carry flags.
15. Boys and girls ride unicycles.
16. The horses wear fancy saddles.
17. The Grand Marshall rides in a convertible.
18. Cindy and Jill sell lemonade.

# Complete That Thought!

ı **action verb** shows what someone or something does.

Example: A cat **meows.**

ll in the circle of the action verb that best completes ıch sentence.

1. When she ________ the car, it ran well.

   ◯ drove ◯ spun ◯ skipped

2. I hope the plane ________ smoothly on our trip.

   ◯ swings ◯ flies ◯ jumps

3. Rosie ________ when she gets hungry.

   ◯ plays ◯ eats ◯ hides

4. In the warm sun, the oranges ________.

   ◯ grew ◯ danced ◯ sang

5. The ocean waves ________ on the beach.

   ◯ ran ◯ splashed ◯ fell

6. The tiny tiger cub ________ as it looked for its mother.

   ◯ barked ◯ laughed ◯ cried

7. Some spiders ________ webs to catch prey.

   ◯ spin ◯ destroy ◯ find

8. The horse ________ through the meadow.

   ◯ galloped ◯ swam ◯ floats

9. The crowd ________ for its favorite team.

   ◯ gathered ◯ competed ◯ cheers

# Action!

An action verb is a word that names an action.

Example: The dog barked.

Underline the action verb in each sentence.

1. I ate a tuna salad sandwich for lunch.
2. The earth spins on its axis.
3. Will you read me the story about the three bears?
4. The bat flew rapidly through the air.
5. Planes fly at a high altitude.
6. Bernadette sang a song for the school talent show.
7. The cat jumped onto my lap.
8. The children play baseball at Secor Park.
9. Antonio kicked the soccer ball into the goal.
10. Kera stretches her arms and legs.

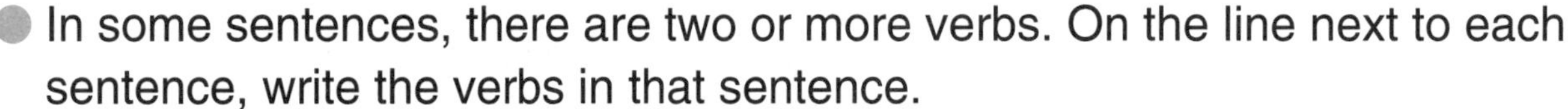

In some sentences, there are two or more verbs. On the line next to each sentence, write the verbs in that sentence.

11. We jumped and skipped at school. ________________________
12. I hate to eat and run. ________________________
13. The sunlight danced and sparkled on the waves. ________________________
14. My empty stomach churned and growled. ________________________
15. Lisa hit the ball and ran to first base. ________________________
16. Steven swims and dives. ________________________

# In Place

pronoun is a word that takes the place of one or more nouns.

Example: **Kristin** ate an apple.
**She** ate an apple.

ome pronouns are listed in the box below.

**Word Box**

| he | she | they | we | his |
|---|---|---|---|---|
| him | her | them | us | it |

Vrite the pronoun that replaces the **purple** noun. Use words in the Word Box.

_______________ 1. **Jeff** ate a hot dog at the baseball game.

_______________ 2. I enjoy eating **cotton candy** at the circus.

_______________ 3. **Kate** will come and visit in July.

_______________ 4. Juan wants to ride on **Jennifer's** horse.

_______________ 5. **Heidi and Jamie** rode the elephant.

_______________ 6. **Tom's** car was stolen from the parking garage.

_______________ 7. Julius gave **Tony** the book to read.

_______________ 8. Beth borrowed **Amy's** hockey stick.

_______________ 9. **The book** fell off the shelf.

_______________ 10. **The computer** constantly breaks down.

_______________ 11. **Louis and I** will go to the amusement park on Saturday.

_______________ 12. Anita found **shells** on the beach.

_______________ 13. Lucas took **Serina and me** to the concert.

# Choose One

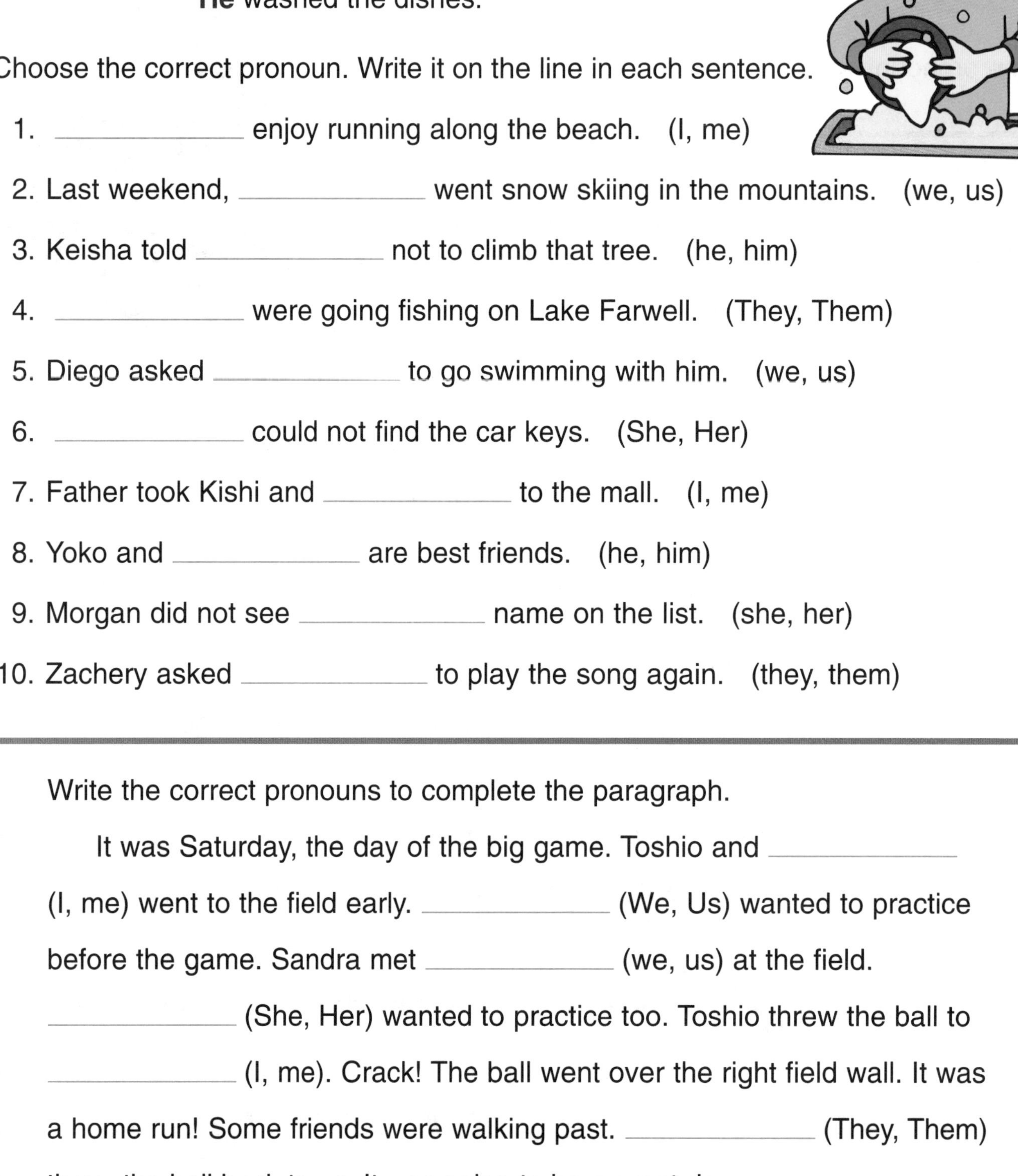

A **pronoun** is a word that can take the place of nouns.

Example: **Joaquin** washed the dishes.
**He** washed the dishes.

Choose the correct pronoun. Write it on the line in each sentence.

1. ____________ enjoy running along the beach. (I, me)
2. Last weekend, ____________ went snow skiing in the mountains. (we, us)
3. Keisha told ____________ not to climb that tree. (he, him)
4. ____________ were going fishing on Lake Farwell. (They, Them)
5. Diego asked ____________ to go swimming with him. (we, us)
6. ____________ could not find the car keys. (She, Her)
7. Father took Kishi and ____________ to the mall. (I, me)
8. Yoko and ____________ are best friends. (he, him)
9. Morgan did not see ____________ name on the list. (she, her)
10. Zachery asked ____________ to play the song again. (they, them)

Write the correct pronouns to complete the paragraph.

It was Saturday, the day of the big game. Toshio and ____________ (I, me) went to the field early. ____________ (We, Us) wanted to practice before the game. Sandra met ____________ (we, us) at the field. ____________ (She, Her) wanted to practice too. Toshio threw the ball to ____________ (I, me). Crack! The ball went over the right field wall. It was a home run! Some friends were walking past. ____________ (They, Them) threw the ball back to us. It was going to be a great day.

# Let's Describe It

n **adjective** is a word that describes a un or a pronoun. An adjective tells hat kind or how many.

Cindy has a **green** frog.

Write one adjective to describe each noun.

1. flower ______________
2. lions ______________
3. pizza ______________
4. breeze ______________
5. boat ______________
6. bike ______________
7. bedroom ______________
8. table ______________
9. clown ______________
10. ocean ______________
11. forest ______________
12. sun ______________

Underline the adjectives in each sentence.

13. It was a warm, humid summer day.
14. Jordan went swimming in the cool water.
15. The private lake was surrounded by tall trees.
16. He swam to a large raft in the middle of the lake.
17. Jordan dove off of the old, rickety diving board.
18. He felt a cool breeze as he surfaced.
19. Two friends joined him on the raft.
20. Yitzi was wearing his green and blue swimsuit.
21. Daniel had brought his new goggles.
22. They lounged in the hot sun telling funny jokes.

# Many Adjectives Here!

An adjective is a word that describes, or tells more about, a noun. An adjective is often found in front of the noun it describes. Example: The large parrot talks.

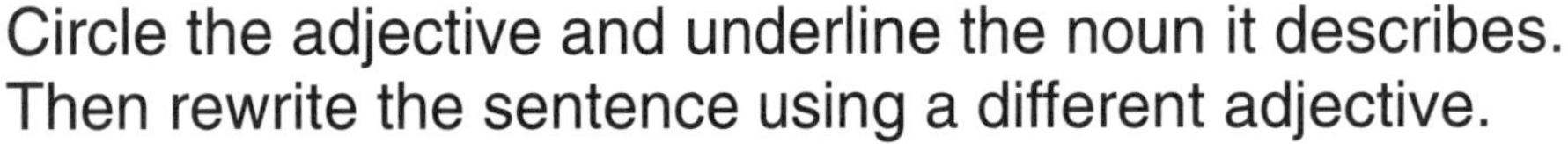

Circle the adjective and underline the noun it describes. Then rewrite the sentence using a different adjective.

1. The ferocious bear wandered into our camp.

   ______________________________

2. Yoshi walked through the chilly room.

   ______________________________

3. The powerful wind blew my umbrella inside out!

   ______________________________

4. The intelligent girl was the winner of the game.

   ______________________________

5. The crows ate the delicious strawberries.

   ______________________________

6. The colorful fish ate food from my hand.

   ______________________________

7. The small cats were chasing the dogs.

   ______________________________

8. The musicians wore silk jackets.

   ______________________________

# Commas Galore

**comma** is used between the day and year in a date.
ommas are used in a list of three or more words in a sentence.

Examples: I went fishing on June 5, 1994.

I live with a dog, a cat, and a bird.

Underline the sentences that use commas correctly.

1. Bring me a pencil, a paper clip, an eraser, and a book.
2. Once I saw a bear, three cubs, a deer, and a raccoon.
3. Leon was born on May 12, 1984.
4. Lenia had a doctor's appointment on September 4 1996.
5. I ate a salad a roll, and a cookie for lunch.
6. Soccer baseball and football are fun to play.
7. Did you wash your face, brush your teeth, and comb your hair?
8. Natalie had her birthday party on August 17 1995.

Add commas where they belong in each sentence.

9. Mother needs to buy lettuce carrots cucumbers and mushrooms.
10. The monkey snake and butterfly live in the jungle.
11. The book report is due on April 14 1997.
12. A triathlete must swim bike and run.
13. Maria had a dentist appointment on December 5 1996.
14. My grandfather was born on March 23 1940.
15. Halina likes to read jump rope swing and play chess.

# Beginning and Ending

A sentence begins with a capital letter. It ends with a punctuation mark.

A **statement** ends with a period.
Example: I see an elephant.

A **question** ends with a question mark.
Example: Did you see that elephant?

An **exclamation** ends with an exclamation mark.
Example: Wow, that's a huge elephant!

Begin and end each sentence correctly. Write the sentence on the line.

1. where are you going

______________________________

2. i am going mountain climbing

______________________________

3. do you like to climb mountains

______________________________

4. yes, I enjoy the challenge of climbing mountains

______________________________

5. would you like to go mountain climbing with me

______________________________

6. wow, that would be great

______________________________

7. remember to bring a canteen of water

______________________________

8. hurrah, I am going to climb a mountain

______________________________

# At the Beach

efore writing, a writer lists words or phrases bout the topic. If the writer will be writing about e beach, he or she may list *sand, waves, hot, mmer, sun*. Using these words, he or she writes sentence, such as *The hot summer sun beat own on the sand.*

/rite complete sentences that include the words on each sun.

1. ______________________________

2. ______________________________

3. ______________________________

4. ______________________________

# Space Place

Space travelers from another galaxy can say many words, but do not speak in sentences yet. Write complete sentences that include the space travelers' words.

1. Earth has many big trees.

2. ______

3. ______

4. ______

5. ______

# About You

paragraph has a main idea. In many paragraphs, e main idea is stated in one sentence. The other entences give details that support the main idea.

**I love springtime**. The weather is warm, but not hot. The birds all seem to be making nests or feeding babies. Wildflowers bloom. I play outside more now that the snow is gone.

ll of the sentences after **I love springtime** support is main idea.

elow are several main idea sentences about you. For each one, write three entences supporting the main idea.

1. My friend and I have a great time. ____________________

2. There is one food I don't like. ____________________

3. Sometimes I daydream. ____________________

# The Princess and the Prince

A **paragraph** is a group of sentences that tell about one idea. A narrative paragraph tells a story. Fairy tales are a kind of narrative.

Write a narrative paragraph on the lines below about a princess who outsmarts a mean dragon and saves a prince. Remember to use the following writing rules:

1. Write a topic sentence that tells what the paragraph is about.
2. Indent the first sentence.
3. Begin each sentence with a capital letter.
4. End each sentence with a punctuation mark.
5. End the paragraph with a concluding sentence.

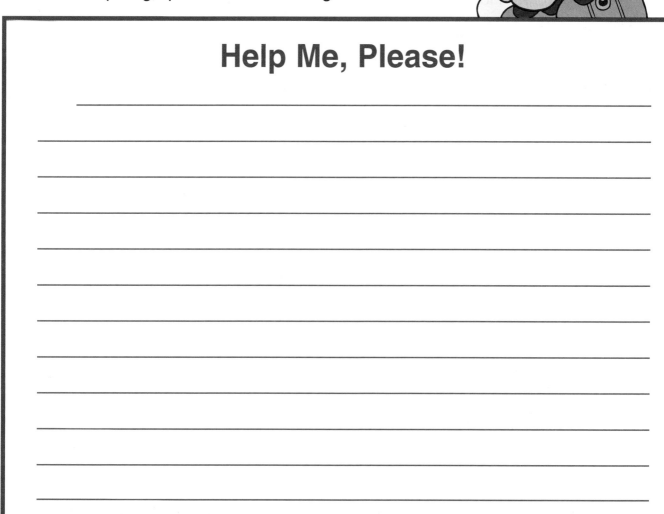

## Help Me, Please!

# Mother and Father, May I?

**paragraph** is a group of sentences that tells about a ain idea. A persuasive paragraph uses details to help onvince someone of something.

hink of something you would like to persuade your arents to do. Write a persuasive paragraph. Remember indent the first word in the paragraph and use correct apitalization and punctuation.

# Alike and Different

Draw a tree and a flower. Think about the tree and the flower. Write three ways they are alike and three ways they are different.

Draw a cat and a dog. Think about the cat and the dog. Write three ways they are alike and three ways they are different.

# Sea Creatures

the reports below, look for the following problems:

- spelling
- capitalization
- punctuation
- misused words

ead the reports and circle the five mistakes in each one. Rewrite each report orrectly on the lines.

The octopus is a see animal. It lives in the pacific Ocean and the Atlantic Oshun. The octopus has ate arms. it changes color when it gets excited.

an interesting feature on a starfish is its arms. The arms help the starfish sea. The starfish can regrow an arm if one is broken of. Under each arm their is a double row of small movable tubes?

# Petition to the Principal

The students at Bear Branch School want new playground equipment. Here is a letter they have written to the principal. Correct the letter. Look for misused words and capitalization, punctuation, and spelling mistakes. (Hint: There are 12 mistakes.

february 15, 1997

Deer Mr. Smith,

We are in need of new playground equipmnt. ours is old and broke. The chanes on the swings is broken. the slide has a crack. They're are no rims on the basketba backboards, and the middle monkey bar is bent. the sandbox is empty, and all the four-square balls have holes? We promise to take car of our new equipment.

Sincerely,
The Students

# Poems Are Fun

ne way to start a poem is to think of a subject. Use the subject as a title and write a pic sentence about it. On each line, write several short sentences that describe and ıpport the topic sentence. These sentences do not need to rhyme. End the poem ith a final thought.

nish writing the free verse poems. In the last box, write your own free verse poem.

**Kittens**

Kittens are playful.
They run.
They jump.
They roll on the floor.
They bite.
They chase.
I love to watch them play.

**Math**

Math is fun!
I can add.
I can subtract.

______________________________

______________________________

Math is my favorite subject!

**Puppies**

I see six puppies.

They are small and furry.

______________________________

______________________________

______________________________

______________________________

I wish they were my puppies.

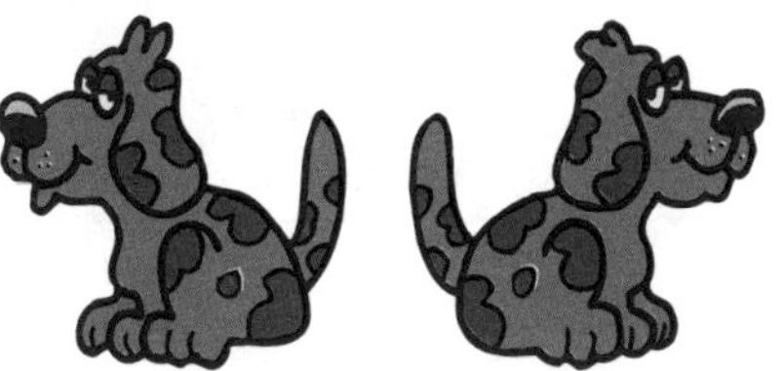

# In a Word

To write an acrostic poem, think of a word and write it going down. Then think of a word, phrase, or sentence that begins with each letter and describes the word. For example:

**I** like to skate on it.
**C**old to touch or taste with my tongue.
**E**veryone likes it in summer.

Notice that this kind of poem does not have to rhyme. It has as many words as you like. Choose one of the words in the word box and write an acrostic poem about it.

| cat | day | hot | wet | fly | car | key |
|---|---|---|---|---|---|---|
| dog | sun | sad | hat | fan | ant | fun |

Write an acrostic poem using the letters in your name or someone else's name.

# Dizzy Directions

ead and follow each set of directions.

| | | |
|---|---|---|
| 1. Put the following numbers in order from smallest to largest: 11, 22, 5, 7 | 2. Draw two circles beside one another. Inside the circle on the right, write the letter *H*. | 3. Draw a solid line from left to right. Above that line, draw a line of dots. Below the solid line, draw a line of dashes. |
| 4. Draw a square. Inside that square, draw a smaller square. Color the smaller square yellow. | 5. On top of each of these hills, draw a circle. Inside each circle, draw a dot. | 6. Write these words in alphabetical order: pour, pool, pond, post |
| 7. Draw a shirt with the following design: short sleeves, up-and-down stripes, six buttons down the front. | 8. Circle the dress with the long sleeves, polka dots, and a frilly hem.    | 9. Write the letters *A*, *B*, and *C* in a row. Put a circle around the A, a square above the B, and a triangle below the C. |

# Can You Follow This?

Read and follow these directions.

1. Color the smaller triangle blue, the circle green, and the larger triangle yellow.

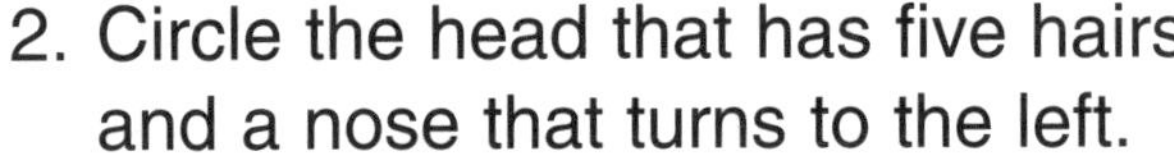

2. Circle the head that has five hairs and a nose that turns to the left.

3. Circle the house that has two windows, a tree on the right, and a chimney on the left.

4. Draw two circles, one inside the other, sitting on top of a square. Under the square, draw a triangle with a corner touching the bottom of the square.

5. Underline the drawing that shows two circles and a triangle. One circle is inside a triangle.

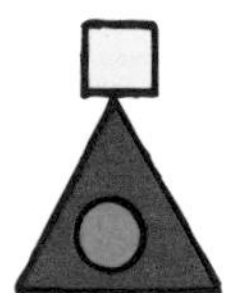

6. Draw a circle inside a square. Put a larger circle on top of the square.

7. Color the circle purple, the triangle red, and the square green.

8. Circle the picture of the bear holding two balloons, riding a bicycle.

# Animals of the World

table of contents lists the chapter titles in a book and the page on which each hapter begins. Using a table of contents can help you find information.

se this table of contents to answer the questions below.

**Animals of the World**



1. On what page could you begin reading about birds?

2. Name the chapter in which you could read about tigers.

3. To what page would you turn to begin reading about animals that lived before books were written?

4. In what chapter could you most likely read about the differences between two kinds of elephants?

5. What chapter begins on page 18?

6. On what page does Swimming Mammals end?

# How to Get There

A table of contents lists information about what is in a book.

### Table of Contents



Answer each question by using the table of contents above. Fill in the correct answer.

| | True | False | Can't tell |
|---|---|---|---|
| 1. To find out places to see, I should turn to page 91. | ○ | ○ | ○ |
| 2. If I like to take my time getting somewhere, I should begin reading on page 71. | ○ | ○ | ○ |
| 3. Flying is my least favorite way to travel. I could skip the chapter beginning on page 1. | ○ | ○ | ○ |
| 4. *On Land* ends on page 31. | ○ | ○ | ○ |
| 5. If I do not like to fly, I should read the chapters that begin on pages 11 and 31. | ○ | ○ | ○ |
| 6. If I like to get to places quickly, I should read the chapter beginning on page 71. | ○ | ○ | ○ |
| 7. The Statue of Liberty is interesting to see. | ○ | ○ | ○ |
| 8. *On the Water* ends on page 30. | ○ | ○ | ○ |
| 9. *Sightseeing* ends on page 154. | ○ | ○ | ○ |

# In Its Place

thesaurus lists words that have similar meanings.

ircle a word in each row that has a similar meaning to
e **red** word. Use the thesaurus below.

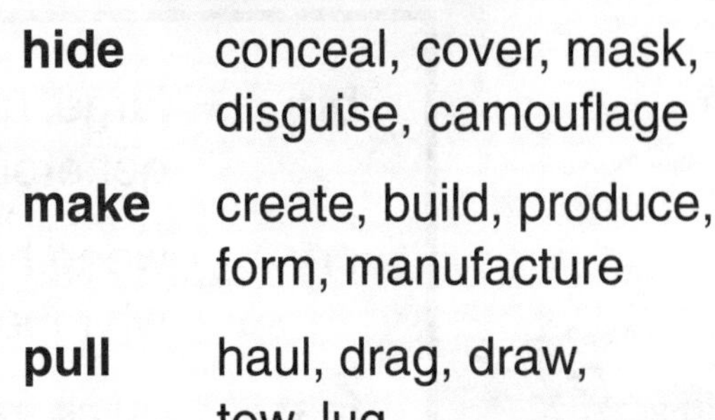

| | | | |
|---|---|---|---|
| **sleep** | slumber, doze, nap, snooze, drowse | **hide** | conceal, cover, mask, disguise, camouflage |
| **slow** | leisurely, unhurried, plodding, lazy | **make** | create, build, produce, form, manufacture |
| **talk** | converse, confer, chat, gossip, discuss | **pull** | haul, drag, draw, tow, lug |

| | | | | |
|---|---|---|---|---|
| . **make** | destroy | produce | demolish | wipe out |
| 2. **sleep** | walk | snooze | awake | busy |
| 3. **pull** | push | thrust | haul | shove |
| 4. **hide** | exhibit | reveal | show | disguise |
| 5. **slow** | fast | plodding | lively | swift |
| 6. **talk** | listen | silence | chat | employ |

Fill in each blank with a clearer, more interesting word. Use the thesaurus above.

7. We will ____________________ with the other team about rescheduling the game.
talk

8. Please ____________________ the bread dough into a circle.
make

9. Mom will ____________________ Dad's birthday gifts in the attic.
hide

# A Clearer Image

A thesaurus lists words that have similar meanings.
It can help make your writing more exact and interesting.

Rewrite each sentence. Replace the blue word with a clearer, more interesting word. Use the thesaurus below.

| | | | |
|---|---|---|---|
| **big** | large, great, massive, generous, huge | **happy** | cheerful, merry, jolly, blithe, gleeful, glad |
| **cry** | weep,bawl, wail, sob whimper | **nice** | pleasant, enjoyable, lovely, acceptable |
| **fast** | quick, rapid, speedy, swift, express | **pretty** | beautiful, good-looking handsome, attractive |

1. Did the puppy cry when we left?

______________________________

2. We had a nice day at the park.

______________________________

3. I would like a big glass of milk.

______________________________

4. There were pretty flowers on each table.

______________________________

5. She will have a fast recovery.

______________________________

6. The happy baby was always smiling.

______________________________

# The ABC's of Dictionaries

here are two guide words at the top of each dictionary page. They show you the first nd last words listed on that page. The rest of the words on the page fall in lphabetical order between the guide words.

retend each list of words is from a page of a dictionary. Write the words in lphabetical order. Circle the words that would be guide words for that page.

neon
needle
observe
number
oath
octopus
only
nurse
notch
owl

thread
tiger
seal
skunk
strawberry
taxi
soap
torch
stingray
television

# These Words Will Guide You

There are two guide words at the top of each dictionary page. They show you the fir and last words listed on that page. The rest of the words fall in alphabetical order between the guide words.

Use the guide words on the pages below to decide where the animal names belong. Write the animal names on the correct page.

| | | | |
|---|---|---|---|
| parrot | cheetah | lynx | yak |
| dolphin | fox | platypus | gibbon |
| beaver | ostrich | cow | eagle |
| anteater | jaguar | llama | hummingbird |

# Letters and Numbers

n encyclopedia is a set of reference books. Each book has a number and a letter on s spine, or side. The letter on each book tells you that topics beginning with that tter are inside. Pictured here is a set of encyclopedias to use as a guide to answer e questions on this page.

ead each sentence. Underline the topic. Write the number of the volume in which ou would find this topic.

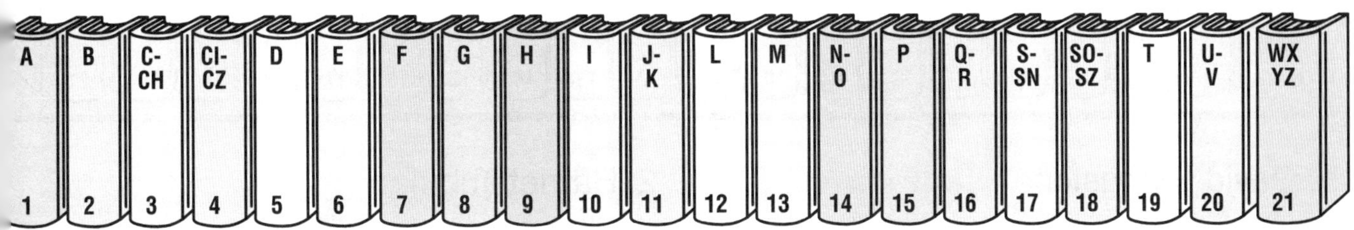


| | | |
|---|---|---|
| 1. What is a geyser? ________ | 2. How many legs does a spider have? ________ | 3. What is a nova? ________ |
| 4. Who invented the telephone? ________ | 5. What is an agouti? ________ | 6. What is the tallest tree? ________ |
| 7. Where did Velcro come from? ________ | 8. What are the primary colors? ________ | 9. What is the capital of Ecuador? ________ |
| 10. What is the population of China? ________ | 11. How is glass made? ________ | 12. What is a quetzal? ________ |

# Last Is Sometimes First

In an encyclopedia, topics are listed in alphabetical order. People are listed with thei last name first, followed by their first name. (Example: Smith, John)

Rewrite each name as it would be listed in the encyclopedia. Then write the number of the encyclopedia volume in which you would find this name.

| A | B | C-CH | CI-CZ | D | E | F | G | H | I | J-K | L | M | N-O | P | Q-R | S-SN | SO-SZ | T | U-V | WX YZ |
|---|---|---|---|---|---|---|---|---|---|---|---|---|---|---|---|---|---|---|---|---|
| 1 | 2 | 3 | 4 | 5 | 6 | 7 | 8 | 9 | 10 | 11 | 12 | 13 | 14 | 15 | 16 | 17 | 18 | 19 | 20 | 21 |

1. David Livingstone

______________________________

volume __________

2. Harriet Tubman

______________________________

volume __________

3. Bessie Colman

______________________________

volume __________

4. Albert Einstein

______________________________

volume __________

5. Claude Monet

______________________________

volume __________

6. Diego Rivera

______________________________

volume __________

7. Marie Curie

______________________________

volume __________

8. Sarah Winnemucca

______________________________

volume __________

# Notes on Australia

When you take notes on what you read, write down only the most important ideas, using the fewest words possible. You don't need to write complete sentences.

Read the paragraph describing Australia.
Then finish the notes below.

Australia is the only country that is also a continent. It is located in the Southern Hemisphere between the Indian and South Pacific oceans. There are long sandy beaches, grassy farmlands, mountains, and much dry sandy desert. In Australia the winter months are June, July, and August. Summer is in December, January, and February. The national capital is in Canberra, and the largest city is Sydney. Kangaroos, koalas, wallabies, wombats, and platypuses are some animals that are native to Australia. Eucalyptus and wattle trees are the most common plants found throughout Australia. Australia is known for its large open spaces, warm and sunny climate, large number of sheep and cattle, and unusual wildlife.

1. Capital ______________________________
2. Largest City ______________________________
3. Location ______________________________
4. Land ______________________________
5. Summer months ______________________________
6. Winter months ______________________________
7. Animals ______________________________

______________________________

8. Plants ______________________________

# Carry Over

Sometimes when you add, you must regroup.

| Add the ones. Regroup. | Add the tens. Regroup. | Add the hundreds. |
|---|---|---|
| $\begin{array}{r} {}^{1}\\ 546 \\ +\,278 \\ \hline 4 \end{array}$ | $\begin{array}{r} {}^{1\,1}\\ 546 \\ +\,278 \\ \hline 24 \end{array}$ | $\begin{array}{r} {}^{1\,1}\\ 546 \\ +\,278 \\ \hline 824 \end{array}$ |

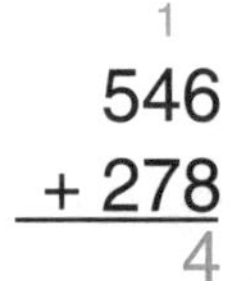

**Add.**

| | | | | |
|---|---|---|---|---|
| 392 + 468 | 264 + 648 | 533 + 269 | 438 + 158 | 384 + 368 |
| 194 + 767 | 256 + 697 | 689 + 157 | 316 + 545 | 388 + 544 |
| 369 + 298 | 184 + 398 | 669 + 236 | 147 + 315 | 576 + 89 |
| 255 + 476 | 289 + 563 | 466 + 437 | 635 + 257 | 296 + 656 |
| 286 + 634 | 248 + 175 | 229 + 487 | 382 + 562 | 176 + 765 |
| | | 215 + 399 | 470 + 181 | 545 + 297 |

# Slam Dunk

ometimes when you add, you must regroup.

| dd the ones. egroup. | Add the tens. Regroup. | Add the hundreds. |
|---|---|---|
| 1<br>269<br>+ 196<br>5 | 1 1<br>269<br>+ 196<br>65 | 1 1<br>269<br>+ 196<br>465 |

dd.

| | | | | |
|---|---|---|---|---|
| 188<br>+ 198 | 765<br>+ 108 | 457<br>+ 394 | 242<br>+ 139 | 286<br>+ 278 |
| 528<br>+ 417 | 637<br>+ 192 | 356<br>+ 367 | 189<br>+ 193 | 345<br>+ 460 |
| 381<br>+ 564 | 393<br>+ 185 | 223<br>+ 382 | 183<br>+ 378 | 223<br>+ 189 |
| 406<br>+ 567 | 422<br>+ 286 | 568<br>+ 412 | 277<br>+ 545 | 186<br>+ 179 |
| 463<br>+ 129 | 536<br>+ 248 | 542<br>+ 365 | 285<br>+ 398 | 191<br>+ 277 |
| 176<br>+ 675 | 605<br>+ 175 | 712<br>+ 199 | 159<br>+ 279 | 389<br>+ 296 |

# Borrowing From a Neighbor

Sometimes when you subtract, you must regroup.

| Regroup 6 tens 2 ones as 5 tens and 12 ones. Subtract the ones. | Regroup 4 hundreds 5 tens as 3 hundreds 15 tens. Subtract the tens. | Subtract the hundreds. |
|---|---|---|
| 5 12<br>462<br>− 296<br>6 | 15<br>3 5 12<br>462<br>− 296<br>66 | 15<br>3 5 12<br>462<br>− 296<br>166 |

**Subtract.**

| | | | | |
|---|---|---|---|---|
| 363<br>− 295 | 311<br>− 122 | 841<br>− 578 | 842<br>− 283 | 317<br>− 178 |
| 245<br>− 186 | 641<br>− 169 | 812<br>− 649 | 633<br>− 147 | 952<br>− 574 |
| 414<br>− 199 | 750<br>− 242 | 630<br>− 302 | 725<br>− 246 | 671<br>− 482 |
| 724<br>− 468 | 412<br>− 236 | 741<br>− 597 | 631<br>− 193 | |
| 632<br>− 243 | 752<br>− 365 | 924<br>− 515 | 528<br>− 329 | |

# At the Ball Field

ometimes when you subtract, you must regroup.

egroup 6 tens 3 ones
5 tens and 13 ones.
ubtract the ones.

Regroup 4 hundreds 5 tens as 3 hundreds 15 tens. Subtract the tens.

Subtract the hundreds.

$$\begin{array}{r} \scriptstyle 5\,13 \\ 4\not{6}\not{3} \\ -\,194 \\ \hline 9 \end{array} \qquad \begin{array}{r} \scriptstyle 15 \\ \scriptstyle 3\,\not{5}\,13 \\ \not{4}\not{6}\not{3} \\ -\,194 \\ \hline 69 \end{array} \qquad \begin{array}{r} \scriptstyle 15 \\ \scriptstyle 3\,\not{5}\,13 \\ \not{4}\not{6}\not{3} \\ -\,194 \\ \hline 269 \end{array}$$

**ubtract.**

| | | | |
|---|---|---|---|
| 948 − 579 | 411 − 260 | 526 − 368 | 812 − 645 |
| 623 − 358 | 428 − 161 | 524 − 375 | 865 − 477 |
| 826 − 197 | 384 − 126 | 593 − 287 | 672 − 381 |

**Solve the word problems below.**

1. José threw his ball 211 times this morning. He threw it 186 times this afternoon. How many more times did he throw it this morning than this afternoon?

2. The Green Sox hit 223 home runs last year. This year they hit 199. How many more did they hit last year?

# Let's Volley

**Multiply.**

| | |
|---|---|
| 0 x 4 = ______ | 0 x 6 = ______ |
| 0 x 8 = ______ | 0 x 3 = ______ |
| 0 x 1 = ______ | 0 x 5 = ______ |
| 0 x 9 = ______ | 0 x 7 = ______ |
| 0 x 0 = ______ | 0 x 2 = ______ |

| | |
|---|---|
| 1 x 4 = ______ | 1 x 9 = ______ |
| 1 x 2 = ______ | 1 x 1 = ______ |
| 1 x 8 = ______ | 1 x 6 = ______ |
| 1 x 5 = ______ | 1 x 7 = ______ |
| 1 x 3 = ______ | 1 x 0 = ______ |

| | |
|---|---|
| 2 x 8 = ______ | 2 x 6 = ______ |
| 2 x 3 = ______ | 2 x 9 = ______ |
| 2 x 5 = ______ | 2 x 7 = ______ |
| 2 x 0 = ______ | 2 x 4 = ______ |
| 2 x 1 = ______ | 2 x 2 = ______ |

| | |
|---|---|
| 3 x 0 = ______ | 3 x 5 = ______ |
| 3 x 6 = ______ | 3 x 9 = ______ |
| 3 x 2 = ______ | 3 x 7 = ______ |
| 3 x 8 = ______ | 3 x 1 = ______ |
| 3 x 3 = ______ | 3 x 4 = ______ |

| | |
|---|---|
| 2 x 7 = ______ | 1 x 9 = ______ |
| 3 x 4 = ______ | 0 x 6 = ______ |
| 1 x 8 = ______ | 2 x 2 = ______ |
| 0 x 5 = ______ | 3 x 1 = ______ |

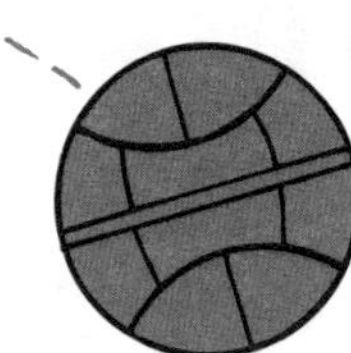

# Soaring With Multiplication

**ultiply.**

| | | | | | | | |
|---|---|---|---|---|---|---|---|
| 3 | 0 | 2 | 3 | | | | |
| x 0 | x 7 | x 6 | x 3 | | | | |
| 3 | 2 | 1 | 2 | | | | |
| x 6 | x 5 | x 8 | x 3 | | | | |
| 2 | 0 | 1 | 3 | | | | |
| x 4 | x 0 | x 7 | x 8 | | | | |
| 1 | 0 | 3 | 2 | | | | |
| x 1 | x 1 | x 9 | x 7 | | | | |
| 3 | 2 | 3 | 1 | | 3 | 2 | 1 |
| x 9 | x 5 | x 6 | x 0 | | x 6 | x 3 | x 5 |
| | | | | 3 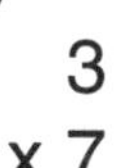 | 2 | 0 | 1 |
| | | | | x 7 | x 2 | x 3 | x 9 |
| | | | 2 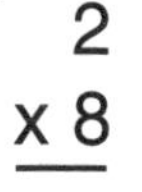 | 1 | 2 | 0 | 0 |
| | | | x 8 | x 3 | x 0 | x 8 | x 9 |
| | | | 3  | 1 | 0 | 3 | 2 |
| | | | x 1 | x 4 | x 4 | x 8 | x 7 |

# What's the Answer?

**Multiply.**

| | | | |
|---|---|---|---|
| A<br>4 x 0 = ______ | E<br>5 x 5 = ______ | I<br>5 x 8 = ______ | M<br>5 x 7 = ______ |
| Q<br>5 x 3 = ______ | U<br>4 x 9 = ______ | B<br>4 x 8 = ______ | F<br>5 x 2 = ______ |
| J<br>5 x 3 = ______ | N<br>4 x 7 = ______ | R<br>4 x 6 = ______ | C<br>5 x 6 = ______ |
| O<br>4 x 2 = ______ | S<br>4 x 5 = ______ | W<br>4 x 4 = ______ | D<br>4 x 3 = ______ |
| L<br>5 x 1 = ______ | T<br>4 x 1 = ______ | K<br>4 x 6 = ______ | G<br>4 x 9 = ______ |

Fill in the correct letter over each answer.

How does an elephant get down from a tree?

___ ___    ___ ___ ___ ___ ___ ___
40 4    30 5 40 35 32 20

___ ___ ___ ___    ___    ___ ___ ___ ___
8 28 4 8    0    5 25 0 10

___ ___ ___    ___ ___ ___ ___ ___
0 28 12    16 0 40 4 20

___ ___ ___ ___    ___ ___ ___ ___ .
4 40 5 5    10 0 5 5

# Racing Multipliers

**ultiply.**

| | | | | | | | |
|---|---|---|---|---|---|---|---|
| 4<br>x 3 | 5<br>x 9 | 5<br>x 5 | 4<br>x 6 | 5<br>x 0 | 4<br>x 2 | 5<br>x 6 | 4<br>x 4 |
| 4<br>x 0 | 5<br>x 7 | 5<br>x 1 | 4<br>x 9 | 4<br>x 1 | 5<br>x 2 | 4<br>x 7 | 5<br>x 8 |
| 4<br>x 8 | 5<br>x 0 | 3<br>x 5 | 4<br>x 2 | 4<br>x 5 | 4<br>x 6 | 5<br>x 4 | 5<br>x 6 |
| 4<br>x 3 | 5<br>x 9 | 4<br>x 5 | 5<br>x 6 | 4<br>x 0 | 5<br>x 2 | 5<br>x 8 | 4<br>x 4 |
| 5<br>x 3 | 5<br>x 8 | 4<br>x 8 | 4<br>x 1 | 5<br>x 0 | 5<br>x 4 | 4<br>x 7 | 5<br>x 7 |
| 5<br>x 3 | 4<br>x 9 | 5<br>x 5 | 4<br>x 6 | 5<br>x 8 | 4<br>x 7 | 4<br>x 9 | 5<br>x 2 |
| 5<br>x 4 | 5<br>x 6 | 4<br>x 7 | 5<br>x 5 | 4<br>x 4 | 4<br>x 2 | 5<br>x 8 | 5<br>x 7 |
| 4<br>x 8 | 4<br>x 4 | 5<br>x 5 | 4<br>x 6 | 5<br>x 3 | 4<br>x 1 | 4<br>x 0 | 4<br>x 3 |

# Sixes and Sevens of Hearts

**Multiply.** In each heart, circle the problem with the greatest product.

| | | | |
|---|---|---|---|
| 6 x 5 = 30 (circled); 7 x 4 = 28 | 6 x 3; 7 x 5 | 7 x 2; 6 x 1 | 7 x 9; 6 x 8 |
| 7 x 6; 6 x 8 | 7 x 1; 6 x 2 | 6 x 9; 7 x 7 | 7 x 2; 6 x 3 |
| 6 x 4; 7 x 4 | 7 x 3; 6 x 7 | 6 x 6; 7 x 8 | 6 x 1; 7 x 1 |
| 7 x 2; 6 x 2 | 6 x 7; 7 x 8 | 7 x 9; 6 x 9 | 7 x 5; 6 x 8 |
| 6 x 5; 7 x 3 | 7 x 7; 6 x 0 | 6 x 6; 7 x 0 | 6 x 4; 7 x 6 |

# Fishing for Facts

**Multiply.**

x 0 = ______ 7 x 7 = ______ 6 x 6 = ______ 7 x 0 = ______

x 1 = ______ 6 x 5 = ______ 7 x 7 = ______ 6 x 9 = ______

x 2 = ______ 7 x 3 = ______ 6 x 3 = ______ 7 x 2 = ______

x 1 = ______ 6 x 9 = ______ 7 x 6 = ______ 6 x 1 = ______

x 4 = ______ 7 x 4 = ______ 6 x 8 = ______ 7 x 9 = ______

7 x 8 = ______ 6 x 0 = ______ 7 x 5 = ______ 6 x 7 = ______

7 x 5 = ______ 6 x 4 = ______ 7 x 9 = ______ 6 x 6 = ______

6 x 2 = ______ 7 x 4 = ______ 6 x 3 = ______ 6 x 5 = ______

7 x 8 = ______ 7 x 2 = ______ 6 x 1 = ______ 6 x 8 = ______

7 x 6 = ______ 6 x 0 = ______ 6 x 7 = ______ 7 x 3 = ______

7 x 0 = ______ 6 x 2 = ______

6 x 9 = ______ 6 x 6 = ______

# Boxcar Patterns

**Multiply.**

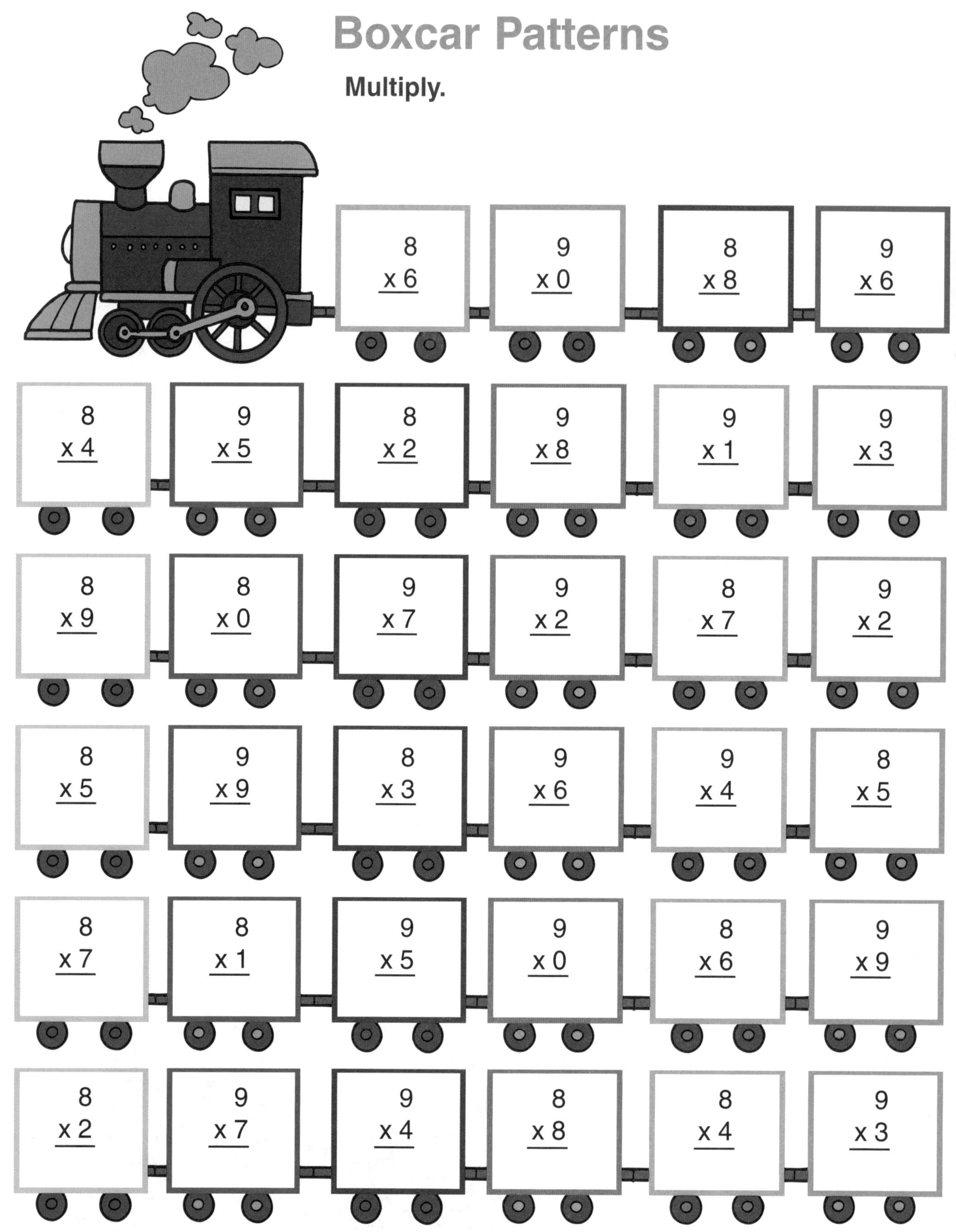

# A Garden of Facts

**ultiply.**

| | | | |
|---|---|---|---|
| x 9 = _____ | 8 x 6 = _____ | 9 x 2 = _____ | 1 x 8 = _____ |
| x 9 = _____ | 9 x 4 = _____ | 8 x 4 = _____ | 9 x 6 = _____ |
| x 0 = _____ | 8 x 8 = _____ | 9 x 3 = _____ | 8 x 5 = _____ |
| x 7 = _____ | 9 x 9 = _____ | 8 x 2 = _____ | 8 x 9 = _____ |
| x 7 = _____ | 8 x 0 = _____ | 9 x 1 = _____ | 8 x 3 = _____ |
| x 5 = _____ | 8 x 6 = _____ | 9 x 2 = _____ | 8 x 1 = _____ |
| x 8 = _____ | 9 x 4 = _____ | 8 x 4 = _____ | 9 x 6 = _____ |
| x 7 = _____ | 9 x 3 = _____ | 8 x 5 = _____ | 9 x 7 = _____ |
| x 3 = _____ | 9 x 1 = _____ | 8 x 8 = _____ | 9 x 8 = _____ |
| x 1 = _____ | 9 x 5 = _____ | 8 x 2 = _____ | 8 x 0 = _____ |
| x 7 = _____ | 9 x 4 = _____ | 8 x 8 = _____ | 9 x 3 = _____ |
| 8 x 9 = _____ | 8 x 2 = _____ | 9 x 5 = _____ | 9 x 1 = _____ |
| 9 x 9 = _____ | 8 x 6 = _____ | 9 x 2 = _____ | 8 x 0 = _____ |
| 9 x 6 = _____ | 8 x 7 = _____ | | |
| 8 x 4 = _____ | 9 x 8 = _____ | | |
| 9 x 8 = _____ | 8 x 5 = _____ | | |

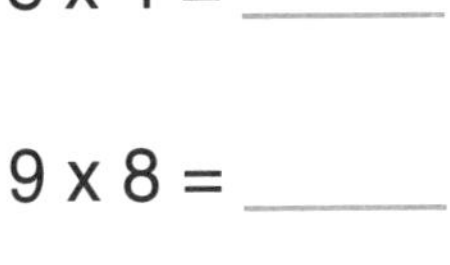

# Dividing Candy

**Divide.**

| | | | |
|---|---|---|---|
| 4 ÷ 2 = ______ | 6 ÷ 3 = ______ | | |
| 10 ÷ 2 = ______ | 8 ÷ 2 = ______ | | |
| 15 ÷ 3 = ______ | 2 ÷ 2 = ______ | 18 ÷ 3 = ______ | 6 ÷ 2 = ______ |
| 3 ÷ 3 = ______ | 18 ÷ 2 = ______ | 16 ÷ 2 = ______ | 12 ÷ 3 = ______ |
| 6 ÷ 2 = ______ | 12 ÷ 3 = ______ | 14 ÷ 2 = ______ | 8 ÷ 2 = ______ |
| 12 ÷ 2 = ______ | 0 ÷ 2 = ______ | 27 ÷ 3 = ______ | 21 ÷ 3 = ______ |
| 9 ÷ 3 = ______ | 18 ÷ 2 = ______ | 24 ÷ 3 = ______ | 0 ÷ 3 = ______ |
| 3 ÷ 3 = ______ | 12 ÷ 2 = ______ | 10 ÷ 2 = ______ | 15 ÷ 3 = ______ |
| 14 ÷ 2 = ______ | 9 ÷ 3 = ______ | 21 ÷ 3 = ______ | 16 ÷ 2 = ______ |
| 4 ÷ 2 = ______ | 6 ÷ 3 = ______ | 27 ÷ 3 = ______ | 2 ÷ 2 = ______ |
| 0 ÷ 3 = ______ | 6 ÷ 2 = ______ | 24 ÷ 3 = ______ | 12 ÷ 3 = ______ |
| 15 ÷ 3 = ______ | 2 ÷ 1 = ______ | 10 ÷ 2 = ______ | 18 ÷ 3 = ______ |
| 3 ÷ 1 = ______ | 18 ÷ 2 = ______ | 9 ÷ 3 = ______ | 12 ÷ 3 = ______ |

# Think and Divide

**…ivide.**

| | | | | |
|---|---|---|---|---|
| $\overline{)6}$ | $2\overline{)4}$ | $3\overline{)24}$ | $3\overline{)3}$ | $3\overline{)21}$ |
| $\overline{)15}$ | $3\overline{)9}$ | $2\overline{)10}$ | $2\overline{)14}$ | $1\overline{)3}$ |
| $\overline{)12}$ | $3\overline{)3}$ | $3\overline{)12}$ | $2\overline{)16}$ | $3\overline{)27}$ |
| $\overline{)2}$ | $1\overline{)2}$ | $3\overline{)18}$ | $2\overline{)6}$ | $2\overline{)18}$ |
| $3\overline{)0}$ | $2\overline{)8}$ | $2\overline{)0}$ | $2\overline{)16}$ | $3\overline{)12}$ |

| | | | |
|---|---|---|---|
| $10 \div 2 =$ 5 | $12 \div 3 =$ ____ | $6 \div 2 =$ ____ | $2 \div 2 =$ ____ |
| $9 \div 3 =$ ____ | $8 \div 2 =$ ____ | $18 \div 3 =$ ____ | $12 \div 2 =$ ____ |
| $18 \div 2 =$ ____ | $6 \div 3 =$ ____ | $14 \div 2 =$ ____ | $3 \div 3 =$ ____ |
| $15 \div 3 =$ ____ | $16 \div 2 =$ ____ | $4 \div 2 =$ ____ | $12 \div 3 =$ ____ |
| $27 \div 3 =$ ____ | $24 \div 3 =$ ____ | | |
| $21 \div 3 =$ ____ | $16 \div 2 =$ ____ | | |
| $18 \div 2 =$ ____ | $6 \div 3 =$ ____ | | |

# Hiking Through Division

**Divide.**

| | | | | |
|---|---|---|---|---|
| $4\overline{)28}$ | $5\overline{)10}$ | $4\overline{)16}$ | | |
| $5\overline{)15}$ | $4\overline{)20}$ | $5\overline{)45}$ | | |
| $4\overline{)24}$ | $5\overline{)40}$ | $4\overline{)12}$ | | |
| $5\overline{)5}$ | $4\overline{)36}$ | $5\overline{)20}$ | $4\overline{)8}$ | $5\overline{)45}$ |
| $5\overline{)30}$ | $4\overline{)4}$ | $4\overline{)16}$ | $4\overline{)32}$ | $4\overline{)4}$ |
| $5\overline{)35}$ | $4\overline{)32}$ | $5\overline{)45}$ | $4\overline{)20}$ | $5\overline{)15}$ |
| $4\overline{)28}$ | $4\overline{)12}$ | $4\overline{)28}$ | $1\overline{)5}$ | $4\overline{)36}$ |

| | | | |
|---|---|---|---|
| 4 ÷ 4 = ____ | 40 ÷ 5 = ____ | 28 ÷ 4 = ____ | 10 ÷ 5 = ____ |
| 30 ÷ 5 = ____ | 8 ÷ 4 = ____ | 25 ÷ 5 = ____ | 12 ÷ 4 = ____ |
| 24 ÷ 4 = ____ | 20 ÷ 5 = ____ | 36 ÷ 4 = ____ | 35 ÷ 5 = ____ |
| 40 ÷ 5 = ____ | 16 ÷ 4 = ____ | 20 ÷ 5 = ____ | 10 ÷ 5 = ____ |
| 35 ÷ 5 = ____ | 24 ÷ 4 = ____ | 36 ÷ 4 = ____ | 20 ÷ 4 = ____ |

# Mystery Boxes

Fill in the missing numbers in each chart by dividing.

| ÷ | 5 |
|---|---|
| 30 | 6 |
| 15 | 3 |
| 45 | |
| 20 | |

| ÷ | 4 |
|---|---|
| 20 | |
| 4 | |
| 16 | |
| 32 | |

| ÷ | 5 |
|---|---|
| 25 | |
| 5 | |
| 40 | |
| 10 | |

| ÷ | 4 |
|---|---|
| 24 | |
| 8 | |
| 36 | |
| 12 | |

| ÷ | 4 |
|---|---|
| 28 | |
| 36 | |
| 16 | |
| 4 | |

| ÷ | 5 |
|---|---|
| 45 | |
| 10 | |
| 25 | |
| 35 | |

| ÷ | 4 |
|---|---|
| 8 | |
| 32 | |
| 24 | |
| 12 | |

| ÷ | 5 |
|---|---|
| 5 | |
| 20 | |
| 15 | |
| 25 | |

| ÷ | 5 |
|---|---|
| 45 | |
| 5 | |
| 20 | |
| 35 | |

| ÷ | 5 |
|---|---|
| 40 | |
| 30 | |
| 10 | |
| 15 | |

| ÷ | 4 |
|---|---|
| 32 | |
| 20 | |
| 12 | |
| 4 | |

# Riding the Rapids

**Divide.**

| | | | |
|---|---|---|---|
| 12 ÷ 6 = ______ | 21 ÷ 7 = ______ | 36 ÷ 6 = ______ | 49 ÷ 7 = ______ |
| 30 ÷ 6 = ______ | 28 ÷ 7 = ______ | 24 ÷ 6 = ______ | 42 ÷ 7 = ______ |
| 48 ÷ 6 = ______ | 63 ÷ 7 = ______ | 56 ÷ 7 = ______ | 54 ÷ 6 = ______ |
| 35 ÷ 7 = ______ | 18 ÷ 6 = ______ | 14 ÷ 7 = ______ | 42 ÷ 7 = ______ |
| 6 ÷ 6 = ______ | 24 ÷ 6 = ______ | 7 ÷ 7 = ______ | 21 ÷ 7 = ______ |
| 54 ÷ 6 = ______ | 35 ÷ 7 = ______ | 63 ÷ 7 = ______ | 42 ÷ 6 = ______ |
| 18 ÷ 6 = ______ | 6 ÷ 6 = ______ | 30 ÷ 6 = ______ | 28 ÷ 7 = ______ |
| 42 ÷ 7 = ______ | 24 ÷ 6 = ______ | 7 ÷ 7 = ______ | 14 ÷ 7 = ______ |

**Divide and write each quotient.**

| | | | | |
|---|---|---|---|---|
| $6\overline{)36}$ | $7\overline{)49}$ | $7\overline{)56}$ | $6\overline{)54}$ | $6\overline{)48}$ |
| $6\overline{)42}$ | $7\overline{)0}$ | $6\overline{)48}$ | $7\overline{)21}$ | $6\overline{)12}$ |
| $7\overline{)35}$ | $6\overline{)6}$ | $7\overline{)42}$ | $7\overline{)14}$ | $6\overline{)18}$ |

# A Camping Trip

olve each word problem.

| | |
|---|---|
| A. The club needs to take 63 pounds of equipment on this trip. How many pounds will each of the 7 hikers need to carry?<br><br>_______ pounds | B. There are 12 hikers. They brought along 6 tents. How many hikers will sleep in each tent?<br><br>_______ hikers |
| C. Seven hikers are hungry. There are 14 oranges. How many oranges can each hiker eat?<br><br>_______ oranges | D. Six hikers need water. They found 54 gallons at their campsite. How many gallons can each hiker have?<br><br>_______ gallons |
| E. There are 42 chores to do to get the camp in order. How many chores does each of the 7 hikers have to do?<br><br>_______ chores | F. Six hikers carry 24 bags of nuts. How many bags will each hiker carry?<br><br>_______ bags |

# Look Who's Dividing

**Divide.**

81 ÷ 9 = ______ 56 ÷ 8 = ______

48 ÷ 8 = ______ 72 ÷ 9 = ______

| | | | |
|---|---|---|---|
| 54 ÷ 9 = ______ | 64 ÷ 8 = ______ | 40 ÷ 8 = ______ | 63 ÷ 9 = ______ |
| 24 ÷ 8 = ______ | 63 ÷ 7 = ______ | 8 ÷ 8 = ______ | 36 ÷ 9 = ______ |
| 72 ÷ 8 = ______ | 45 ÷ 9 = ______ | 16 ÷ 8 = ______ | 32 ÷ 8 = ______ |
| 9 ÷ 9 = ______ | 27 ÷ 9 = ______ | 18 ÷ 9 = ______ | 64 ÷ 8 = ______ |
| 63 ÷ 9 = ______ | 56 ÷ 8 = ______ | 36 ÷ 9 = ______ | 81 ÷ 9 = ______ |
| 32 ÷ 8 = ______ | 16 ÷ 8 = ______ | 40 ÷ 8 = ______ | 72 ÷ 8 = ______ |
| 45 ÷ 9 = ______ | 54 ÷ 9 = ______ | 48 ÷ 8 = ______ | 24 ÷ 8 = ______ |
| 8 ÷ 8 = ______ | 27 ÷ 9 = ______ | 72 ÷ 8 = ______ | 45 ÷ 9 = ______ |
| 9 ÷ 9 = ______ | 18 ÷ 9 = ______ | 40 ÷ 8 = ______ | 72 ÷ 9 = ______ |
| 36 ÷ 9 = ______ | 16 ÷ 8 = ______ | 64 ÷ 8 = ______ | 54 ÷ 9 = ______ |
| 48 ÷ 8 = ______ | 27 ÷ 9 = ______ | 56 ÷ 8 = ______ | 45 ÷ 9 = ______ |

# A Winter Day

**Divide.**

| | | | | |
|---|---|---|---|---|
| $9\overline{)54}$ | $8\overline{)32}$ | $8\overline{)64}$ | $9\overline{)45}$ | $8\overline{)16}$ |
| $9\overline{)72}$ | $9\overline{)27}$ | $9\overline{)81}$ | $8\overline{)56}$ | $9\overline{)63}$ |
| $9\overline{)36}$ | $8\overline{)48}$ | $8\overline{)8}$ | $8\overline{)40}$ | $9\overline{)18}$ |
| $8\overline{)24}$ | $8\overline{)72}$ | $9\overline{)63}$ | $8\overline{)56}$ | $9\overline{)9}$ |

**Solve each word problem.**

**A.** Emily and Matthew made 81 snowmen in 9 days. How many snowmen can they make in one day?

_______ snowmen

**B.** Timmy made 56 snowballs. If he puts the snowballs into 8 piles, how many snowballs will be in each pile?

_______ snowballs

**C.** Pedro made 72 cups of hot chocolate for nine children. If the children drink the same number of cups, how many cups does each child drink?

_______ cups

# Is That All There Is?

Read each of the following paragraphs. After each paragraph is a question. Fill in a circle to explain whether there is enough information to answer the question or not. If there is, answer the question. If there is not, explain what is missing.

1. There are many wildflowers by the side of the road in springtime. It's fun to drive along and look at the beautiful colors. Pink, white, orange, purple, and blue are a few of the colors that make the countryside gorgeous. From deserts to plains to mountains, you can see a wide variety of flowers.

What are the names of some wildflowers you might see in springtime?

◯ Yes, there is enough information to answer the question.

◯ No, there is not enough information to answer the question.

---

2. Some beautiful birds come from Australia. Cockatoos are pink and orange, white and yellow, gray and red, and black. A bird called the rainbow lorikeet is many different colors.

What Australian bird is many different colors?

◯ Yes, there is enough information to answer the question.

◯ No, there is not enough information to answer the question.

---

3. In the wild, dogs and wolves live in packs. There is always a leader of the pack. The pack hunts and eats together.

Where do the packs sleep?

◯ Yes, there is enough information to answer the question.

◯ No, there is not enough information to answer the question.

---

# I Predict

When you make a guess about what will happen next, you are making a **prediction**. Read each story. On the lines below, predict what you think is *most likely* to happen.

1. Sal was sleeping so soundly he did not hear his alarm clock go off. When he woke up, the sun was shining brightly. He rushed to brush his teeth, wash his face, and get dressed. Sal grabbed some fruit to eat for breakfast and ran out the door. Just then, Sal saw a mother cat with four kittens. She looked hungry.

______________________________

______________________________

2. Gina's dog Buttons had been missing for two days. Gina had put up posters all over town with pictures of her dog. She had written *Reward!* on each poster. Gina sat looking out the window, hoping to see Buttons. Suddenly, the phone rang. Mother answered, and then called excitedly, "Gina!"

______________________________

______________________________

3. Maria and Jack love roller coasters, especially those that splash through water. They had stood in line in the summer heat, waiting to get on this one. Now, they were shrieking happily as their car shot up and down the tracks. When the car streaked up to the top of the last hill, they looked down and saw that the tracks led to a huge pond of water!

______________________________

______________________________

# What Is It?

Read each clue carefully. Look at the pictures. Write the name of the animal.

elephant

turtle

porcupine

penguin

blue whale

cheetah

raccoon

lizard

1. I am a mammal. I am huge! My skin is gray. I am the largest land mammal in the world.

   ________________________

2. I have fur. I am a hunter. I am from the cat family. I live in Africa. I run faster than any other kind of cat.

   ________________________

3. I am a reptile. Some people like me to live in their homes because I catch insects. If I am in danger, I may drop off my tail.

   ________________________

4. I am a rodent. I have strong, stiff quills on my back, sides, and tail.

   ________________________

5. I am a furry animal that has a bushy, ringed tail. I have a band of black hair around my eyes that looks like a mask.

   ________________________

6. I am a reptile. I have a shell. I can pull my head, legs, and tail into my shell.

   ________________________

7. I have short, thick feathers and a stocky body. I am a good swimmer. I am a bird, but I can't fly.

   ________________________

8. I live in the ocean. I am a mammal. I am the largest animal that has ever lived.

   ________________________

# Making Comparisons

n analogy is a comparison of things or ideas.

Example: **Rabbit** is to **fast** as **turtle** is to **slow**.

ead and think about each sentence. Choose a word from the Word Box to complete ach sentence.

**Word Box**

| | | | | |
|---|---|---|---|---|
| cold | envelope | cake | sour | huge |
| bottom | bird | bee | light | floating |
| old | tree | hard | | |

1. Velvet is to soft as steel is to ______________________.
2. Summer is to hot as winter is to ______________________.
3. An ant is to tiny as a whale is to ______________________.
4. Bite is to dog as sting is to ______________________.
5. Sugar is to sweet as lemons are to ______________________.
6. Night is to dark as day is to ______________________.
7. A baby is to young as a great grandparent is to ______________________.
8. An airplane is to flying as a boat is to ______________________.
9. Right is to left as top is to ______________________.
10. Swimming is to fish as flying is to ______________________.
11. Cheese is to pizza as frosting is to ______________________.
12. Foot is to sock as letter is to ______________________.
13. Daisy is to flower as oak is to ______________________.

# Cats and Dogs All Over

When solving difficult problems, use the 4-step plan below:

1. Read the entire problem. Understand the question.
2. Decide on a method to solve the problem. Would a list, chart, or picture help?
3. Solve the problem.
4. Check your answer.

Use the 4-step plan to solve these problems.

A. There is a white kitten, a striped kitten, a spotted kitten, and a brown kitten. Eacl kitten is playing with a light blue, green, orange, or dark blue ball of yarn.

- The striped kitten and the spotted kitten are playing with blue yarn.
- The white kitten does not like green.
- The striped kitten only plays with light colors.

Which kitten is playing with which ball of yarn? Use the picture below to help you solve the problem. Color the kittens and balls of yarn.

B. Pat, Quentin, Rosa, Sue, and Tom are walking their dogs.

- Pat's dog is spotted with long ears.
- Rosa's dog does not have long ears or spots.
- Pat's dog does not have a bow.
- Quentin's dog has curly hair.
- Sue's dog is wearing a bow.

Which dog belongs to each owner? Use the picture below to help you solve the problen

# Solving Patterns

hen solving difficult problems, use the 4-step plan below:

. Read the entire problem. Understand the question.
. Decide on a method to solve the problem. Would a list, chart, or picture help?
. Solve the problem.
. Check your answer.

se the grid and the 4-step method to find answers to these questions.

. Amelia needs a flag for her club. She wants to use four shapes: a hexagon ⬢ , a parallelogram ▱, a star ☆, and an oval ⬯ Amelia has drawn a 16-square grid. Use it to help her design her flag. Each row, horizontal and vertical, must have all four shapes in it. There must be no repeats in either direction.

| ⬢ | ▱ | ☆ | ⬯ |
|---|---|---|---|
| | ☆ | | |
| | | ⬢ | |
| | | | ☆ |

B. Keiko and Joseph are building a wall using many different colors of bricks. Can you finish each horizontal row of the wall by following the pattern?

| green | green | red | green | | |
|---|---|---|---|---|---|
| yellow | blue | yellow | blue | yellow | |
| blue | red | blue | | | |
| yellow | green | green | yellow | | |
| red | blue | yellow | red | | |

# Problem Solving Recipe

When solving difficult problems, use the 4-step plan below:

1. Read the entire problem. Understand the question.
2. Decide on a method to solve the problem. Would a list, chart, or picture help?
3. Solve the problem.
4. Check your answer.

A. Sue, Bob, Nick, and Jean each have a different favorite shape—triangle, square, oval, or circle.

- Sue and Nick like straight lines.
- Bob and Sue do not like squares.
- Jean's favorite shape is a circle.
- No two people like the same shape.

What is each person's favorite shape?
Use the chart to help you solve the problem.

| | ▲ (triangle) | ▭ (square) | ⬭ (oval) | ● (circle) |
|---|---|---|---|---|
| Sue | | | | |
| Bob | | | | |
| Nick | | | | |
| Jean | | | | |

B. There are five children standing in line to buy circus tickets. Three are boys—Hector, Bill, and Alonzo. Two are girls—Carla and Alanna.

- Alanna is in front of Hector and Bill.
- Bill is never last.
- No two boys stand next to each other.

Write the order that the children are standing in line.

| ________ | ________ | ________ | ________ | ________ |
|---|---|---|---|---|
| first | second | third | fourth | fifth |

C. There are seven balloons—two are red, three are green, one is yellow, and one is blue. Mia has three balloons. Ted and Cathie each have two balloons.

- Cathie does not have a yellow balloon.
- No child has a blue and a yellow balloon.
- Mia has a blue balloon.
- Each child has a green balloon.

Color each child's balloons the correct color.

# Where Am I?

ometimes we can speculate or guess where a story takes place, based on clues. ead each story below. Under each story is a list of places. If you think the story ould have happened in the place, write **possible** and explain why. If you don't think e story could have happened in the place, write **no** and explain why not.

A. It was dark all around me. It was so dark I could not see my hand without a light. I was cold and wet, too. Suddenly, something alive moved quickly around my head. I reached for it, but missed. The tiny thing darted away. Where was I?

1. in a cave? ____________________
2. in a movie theater? ____________________
3. in an ocean? ____________________

B. There were lights and signs all around me. I could hear sounds of laughter, cries, and screams. I could smell cotton candy, french fries, and taffy. Everywhere I looked, I could see things twirling, spinning, and whooshing up and down. Where was I?

4. at an amusement park? ____________________
5. on the freeway? ____________________
6. at a carnival? ____________________

C. It was hot and sandy. There was a slight breeze. The air smelled of salt water, sweat, and suntan lotion. I could hear the crashing of water against land and rocks, and the squawking of birds. Where was I?

7. at the ski slopes? ____________________
8. at the beach? ____________________
9. at a river? ____________________

# Which Pet?

Read the stories about pets. Write **yes** beside any pet that fits the clues and explain why. Write **no** beside the pets that do not fit the clues and explain why not.

A. Alice has asked for a pet for her birthday. Her family lives in a small, fifth-floor apartment in the middle of a huge city. On the big day, her mother and dad wake her up. Alice sees two long, narrow, fuzzy ears poking out of her mom's pocket. What kind of a pet did Alice get for her birthday?

1. a hamster? ______________________________
2. a puppy? ______________________________
3. a snake? ______________________________
4. a lizard? ______________________________
5. a rabbit? ______________________________

B. On pet day, Chad brings his animal to school. He has asked his classmates to guess what it is. The animal is in a large, clean peanut-butter jar with a lid. Everyone can hear it sing. What might it be?

6. a puppy? ______________________________
7. a cricket? ______________________________
8. a rabbit? ______________________________
9. a gerbil? ______________________________
10. a butterfly? ______________________________

# Take a Trip to the Zoo!

o help us find our way around, we can use a map. The lines on a map form a **grid**. he numbers along the left side and the letters across the bottom of the grid are alled **coordinates**. For example, to find D2, put your finger on D. Move your finger p to 2. Did you find the bat?

Jse the coordinates to find each animal. On the line next to each pair of coordinates, vrite the name of the animal you found there.

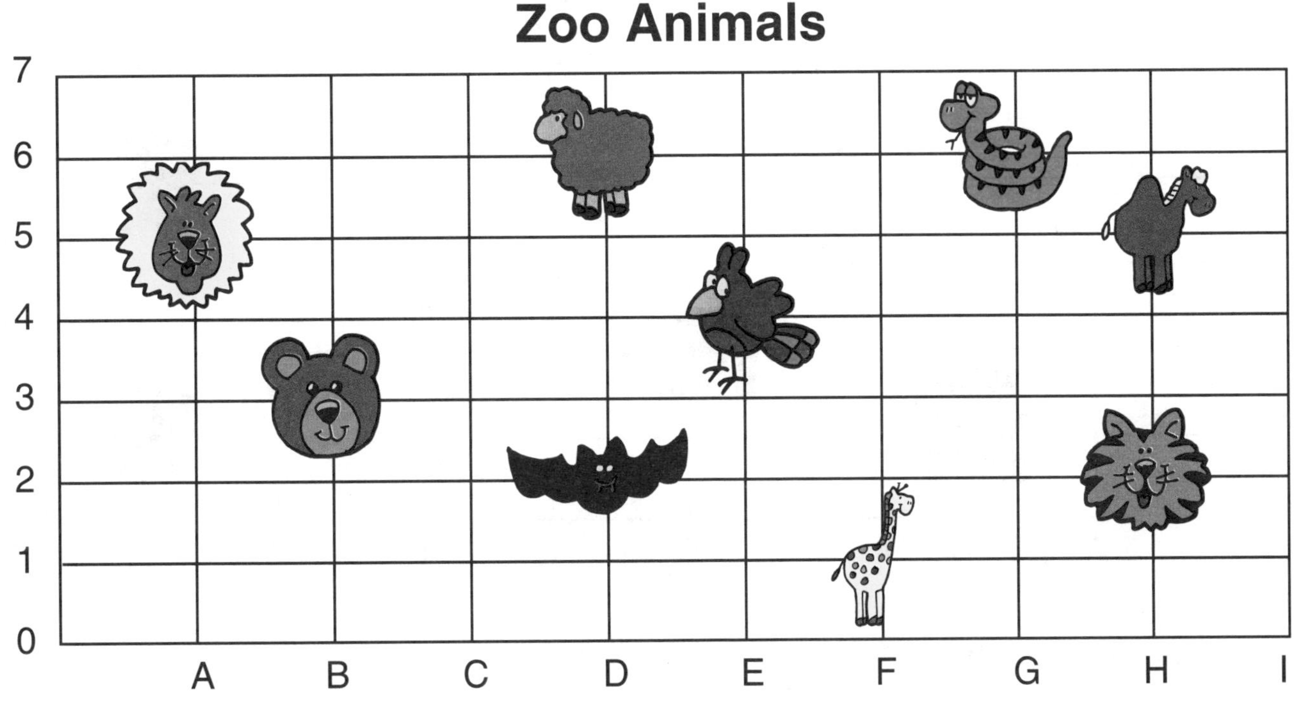


G6 ____________________ B3 ____________________

A5 ____________________ D6 ____________________

H2 ____________________ H5 ____________________

E4 ____________________ F1 ____________________

# On the Farm

The lines on a map form a **grid**. The numbers along the left side and the letters across the bottom of the grid are called **coordinates**. When writing a coordinate, write the letter first and the number second. For example, a cat can be found at E6.

9
8
7
6
5
4
3
2
1
0

A B C D E F G H I

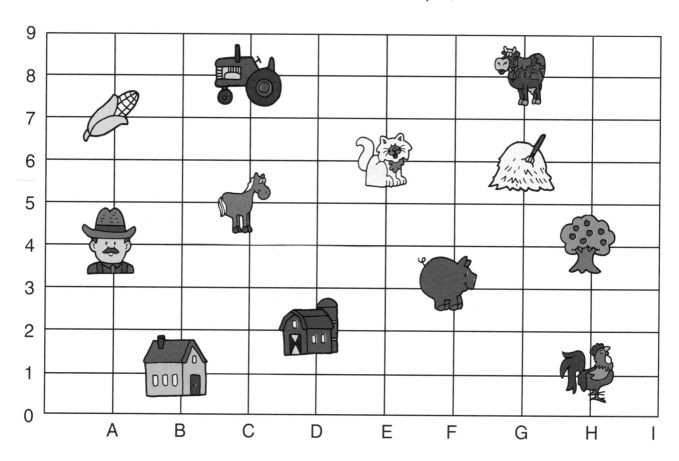

Find each picture on the grid. Write its coordinate.

# Understanding Maps

**ymbols** are drawings that stand for important things on a map. Here are some ymbols you might find on a map.

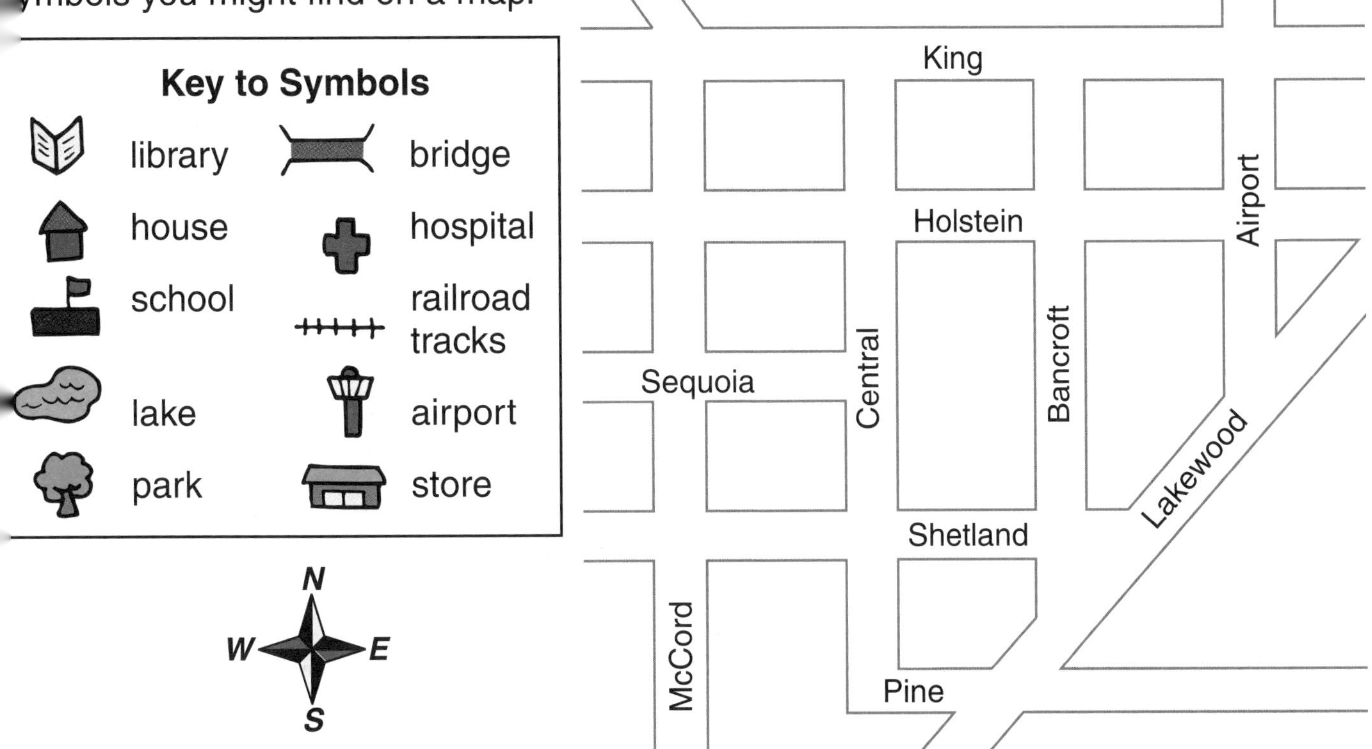


Follow the directions below to draw the correct symbols where they belong on this map.

1. Draw the school symbol on the east side of Bancroft between Holstein and King.
2. Draw the hospital symbol on the south side of King between McCord and Central.
3. Draw the railroad tracks symbol down the middle of Lakewood.
4. Draw the library symbol on the northwest corner of Central and Shetland.
5. Draw the airport symbol on the east corner of Airport and Lakewood.
6. Draw the store symbol on the southwest corner of McCord and Sequoia.
7. Draw the park symbol on the south side of Holstein between Central and Bancroft.
8. Draw the bridge symbol on Pine where it crosses over the railroad tracks.
9. Draw the lake symbol east of Lakewood.

# A Trip to Bear Country

Here is a road map and a legend. The symbols on a map and what they mean are show inside of a **legend**. Looking at the legend will help you read the symbols on a map.

Use the map and legend to answer the questions.

**Legend**

Bear Lake
Grizzly Mountains
river
Bear Cave
Cub School
road
Bear Cub Pool
camping
blueberries

Grizzly Town
N
W
E
S
Kodiak
Bear Junction
Bear Branch Village
Brown Bear Village

1. Where could the bears go camping?____________________
2. What direction would the bears travel to go from the school to the river?
   ____________________
3. In what town do the cubs go to school?____________________
4. Where could the bears pick blueberries?____________________
5. In what town is the pool?____________________
6. If the bears were at the lake, which direction would they travel to get to Bear Branch Village?____________________
7. What direction are the mountains from the cave?____________________
8. What direction is Kodiak from Bear Junction?____________________

# Good Sports

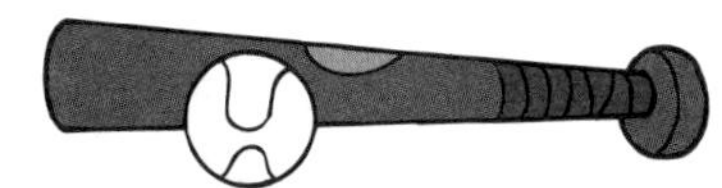

A **bar graph** uses bars to show how much or how many. For example, a bar graph might be used to show how many runs a person scored. For two runs, there would be two bars. You can compare the lengths of the bars to quickly see differences in number.

The bar graph below shows how many runs each person scored in a baseball game. Use the bar graph to answer the questions below.

## Runs Scored in a Baseball Game

| | 0–1 | 1–2 | 2–3 | 3–4 | 4–5 | 5–6 | 6–7 | 7–8 | 8–9 |
|---|---|---|---|---|---|---|---|---|---|
| Mary | ■ | ■ | | | | | | | |
| Jake | ■ | | | | | | | | |
| Sue | ■ | ■ | ■ | ■ | ■ | | | | |
| Jess | ■ | ■ | ■ | ■ | ■ | | | | |
| Sami | ■ | ■ | ■ | | | | | | |
| Mitzi | ■ | ■ | ■ | ■ | ■ | ■ | ■ | ■ | |

0 1 2 3 4 5 6 7 8 9

1. Who scored the least number of runs?____________________
2. Who scored the most runs?____________________
3. How many more runs did Sue score than Mary?____________________
4. Who scored three runs ?____________________
5. Who had the same number of runs?____________________
6. If Sami scores four more runs, how many runs will he have?____________________
7. How many runs did Mary and Jess score altogether?____________________
8. How many players scored more than four runs?____________________
9. Which three children's totals together equal six runs?____________________

________________________________________

# The Lunch Bunch

During one week at Woodside Elementary School, third graders kept track of the kinds of fruit each student brought for lunch. They wanted a quick way to organize and record this information, so they made a picture graph. On a **picture graph**, a small drawing represents each real object. Use this picture graph to answer the questions below.

**Fruit Brought for Lunch by Woodside Third Graders**

| | |
|---|---|
| Bananas | |
| Apples | |
| Pears | |
| Tangerines | |
| Nectarines | |
| Peaches | |
| Oranges | |
| Boxes of raisins | |

1. How many boxes of raisins did the students eat in a week?__________
2. How many more peaches than oranges did they eat?__________
3. What fruit did they eat the most of?__________
4. How many apples, pears, and oranges did they eat altogether?__________
5. What fruit did they eat the least of?__________
6. How many more bananas did they eat than nectarines?__________
7. If they had eaten six more pears, how many would they have eaten?__________
8. Which two fruits together equal twelve?__________
9. Which two fruits did they eat an equal amount of?__________

# How Many Birds at the Feeder?

**line graph** can be used to compare information that is gathered at ifferent times. The line graph below shows the number of birds that ame to Rose and Adam's bird feeder over the past year. Use this graph ɔ answer the questions below.

**Birds**

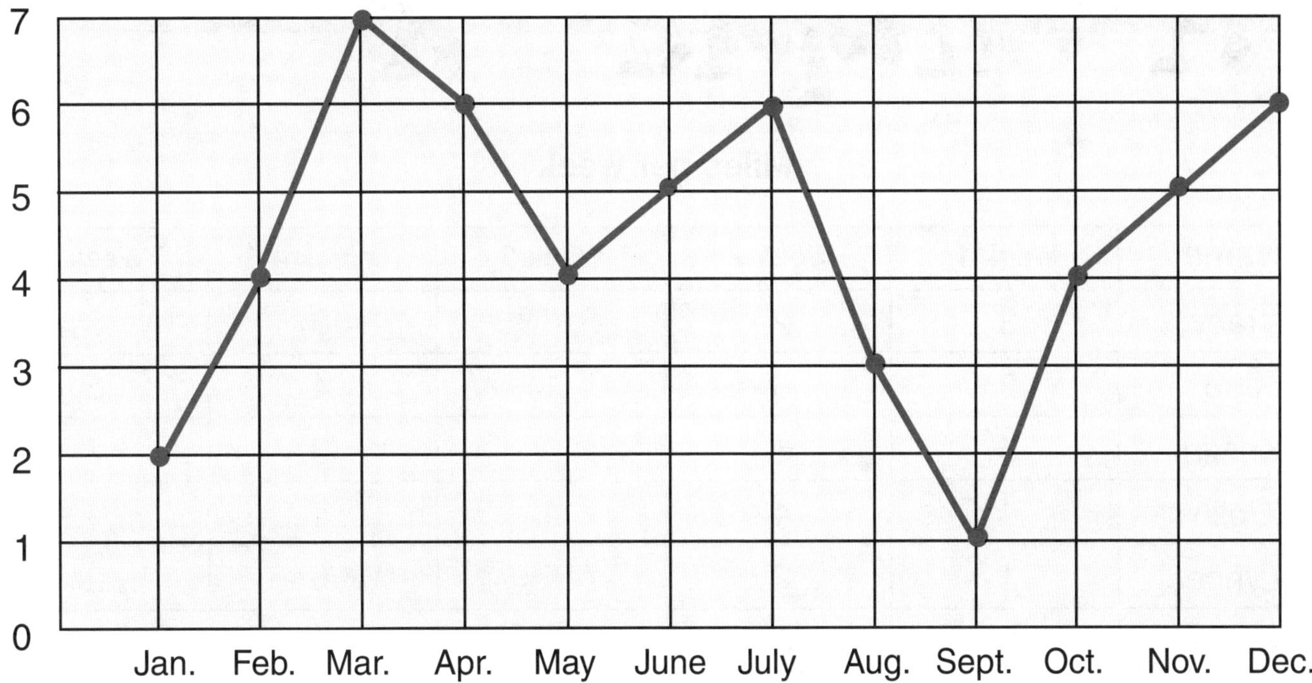


1. In what month did they see the most birds at their feeder? ____________________
2. How many more birds did they see in April than in June? ____________________
3. In what month did the fewest birds come? ____________________
4. How many birds have come to the feeder altogether? ____________________
5. In what month did two birds come? ____________________
6. If five fewer birds had come in July, how many would have been there? __________
7. How many birds altogether came in October and November? ____________________
8. In which month did only three birds come? ____________________

# Charting a Walkathon

At Woodbridge Elementary School, the students held a walkathon. To keep track of each person's weekly progress, a chart was kept. Use the information on this chart t answer the questions below.

**Miles per week**

| Name | Week 1 | Week 2 | Week 3 | Week 4 | Week 5 |
|---|---|---|---|---|---|
| Tracy | 3 | 2 | 4 | 3 | 3 |
| Joe | 2 | 6 | 1 | 4 | 5 |
| Kristin | 5 | 1 | 6 | 3 | 7 |
| Colin | 4 | 4 | 4 | 4 | 4 |
| Lynne | 1 | 2 | 5 | 6 | 2 |
| Dave | 6 | 3 | 2 | 1 | 0 |

1. Which students walked more miles in week two than in week one?____________

________________________________________

2. Which student walked the same distance each week?____________

3. Who walked less each week than the week before?____________

4. Which students walked the same distance in week three?____________

________________________________________

5. Who had walked the farthest by the end of five weeks?____________

6. During which week did the 6 walkers total the greatest distance?____________

7. During which week did they walk the shortest distance?____________

# Answers

**ge One**

photo — 9. coughed
paragraph — 10. rough
telephone — 11. trough
alphabet — 12. gopher
laugh — 13. nephew
graph — 14. orphanage
enough — 15. pheasant
autograph

**ge Two**

flower — 8. crowd
cloud — 9. ounces
outside — 10. growl
howl — 11. around
sound — 12. found
town — 13. loudly
down — 14. bounced

**age Three**

ne following sentences
hould be underlined:
An owl is a kind of bird.
Some animals are reptiles.
People can buy bread at a store.
Chicken is a type of meat.
A pen pal is a person who writes letters.
Some books tell about real people.
7. A spider is an animal with eight legs.

he remaining sentences
hould be circled.

**age Four**

1. fact — 7. opinion
2. fact — 8. opinion
3. opinion — 9. opinion
4. opinion — 10. opinion
5. fact — 11. fact
6. fact — 12. fact

**Page Five**

1. escaped.
2. went in to see the pup.
3. chased the cat.

**Page Seven**

The sentences are numbered in the following order:

4, 2, 3, 1
1, 2, 4, 3
4, 2, 1, 3
4, 3, 2, 1

**Page Eight**

First, get into your blue and red clown costume.
Next, put a makeup cape over your costume.
Make up your face.
Then take off the makeup cape.
Finally, put on a red nose and an orange fuzzy wig and go on stage.

**Page Nine**

1. a statue
2. a musical performance
3. rider
4. a large rock
5. a meeting with someone to get information

**Page Ten**

1. an animal
2. a toy
3. money left over
4. guides in a certain way
5. a kind of bird
6. pass

**Page Eleven**

Word Box—uneven, disorder, disobey, unplug

1. disorder — 5. decamp
2. disobey — 6. deplane
3. uneven — 7. rebuild
4. unplug

**Page Twelve**

Word Box—marvelous, breathless, peaceful, bendable

1. bendable
2. marvelous
3. peaceful
4. breathless
5. courageous
6. dangerous; full of danger
7. timeless; without time
8. treatable; capable of being treated
9. wonderful; full of wonder

**Page Thirteen**

1. 3, 3 — 8. 2
2. 2, 1 — 9. 2
3. 2, 2 — 10. 3
4. 3, 2 — 11. 3
5. 3, 3 — 12. 3
6. 2, 2 — 13. 2
7. 1 — 14. 2

**Page Fourteen**

1. lad der
2. com pound
3. or bit
4. ham mer
5. pub lish
6. en ter
7. ar row
8. cen ter
9. gal lop
10. mus tard
11. 2 — 15. 3
12. 2 — 16. 3
13. 3 — 17. 3
14. 4 — 18. 3

**Page Fifteen**

Circled sentences:

1. Hiking in springtime can be interesting.
2. It's nice to have a pet.
3. Deserts are full of life.
4. Texas is an interesting place.

Remaining sentences should be underlined.

**Page Sixteen**

The following circles should be filled in:

1. all three circles
2. middle and bottom
3. top and middle
4. middle and bottom
5. all three circles

**Page Seventeen**

1. A stranger knocked on the door.
2. He got wet.
3. Adam crept up and tapped her arm.
4. The fire alarm sounded.
5. The candle burned out.
6. The ants ate the food.

**Page Eighteen**

1. Kimbria rides the horse.
2. The dog is hungry.
3. Caitlyn cannot ride the horse.
4. Steve missed his cats.
5. Lynn went skating.
6. Kristen needed gifts.
7. Rick did not have his homework.
   His dog ate it.

**Page Nineteen**

1. leave — 6. kind
2. ate — 7. walked
3. happy — 8. journey
4. hid — 9. helped
5. angry — 10. argued

**Page Twenty**

1. enormous — 5. awkward
2. tiny — 6. graceful
3. tense — 7. eager
4. relaxed — 8. reluctant

**Page Twenty-one**

person—Travis, brother, Maria, firefighter
place—China, school, store, house
thing—hamster, eraser, bike, football

Circled words:

2. picture — 10. car
5. clock — 11. Mice
8. book — 12. net
9. Balls

Underlined words:

1. Linda
3. Grandma
4. Patterson School
6. LaNell
7. Max

**Page Twenty-two**

Words underlined once:

1. country, buildings
2. queen, dogs
4. family, vacation
5. picnic
6. pizza, ice cream
7. heart
8. islands

Words underlined twice:

1. Italy
3. Olympics, Norway, France
4. Grand Canyon
5. Saturday, Wildwood Park
6. Emily, Little Flower School
7. Doctor Smith
9. thing
10. place
11. person
12. thing
13. place
14. thing

# Answers continued

**Page Twenty-three**

1. We
2. The wildflowers
3. All the trees in my neighborhood
4. My favorite tree
5. I
6. One of my friends
7. Our neighborhood club
8. We
9. Mom and Dad
10. They
11. Mom and I
12. The bulbs
13. I
14. My friends and I
15. Jill
16. I

**Page Twenty-four**

1–6: Answers will vary.

7. Alex
8. He
9. Jake and I
10. Alex's sister
11. She
12. Sue's talent
13. Math
14. My favorite fish
15. Tom and Kim
16. The two men
17. My neighbors
18. The library
19. The milk
20. The computer
21. Penguins
22. Steve and Jeremy

**Page Twenty-five**

1. packed a picnic lunch.
2. rode his bike to his friend's house.
3. walked to the park.
4. played baseball.
5. ate peanut butter sandwiches and cookies.
6. climbed on the monkey bars.
7. live in Calgary Canada.
8. build nests in springtime.
9. performs tricks with a rabbit.
10. got a new bike for my birthday.
11. is gray today.
12. sells ice cream.

**Page Twenty-six**

1. gets ready for the parade.
2. build the floats.
3. practices every day.
4. sound fantastic.
5. groom their horses.
6. practice their tricks.
7. hang up flags.
8. line up along the sidewalks.
9. goes down Main Street.
10. sway back and forth to the beat.
11. wear tall hats.
12. throw and catch their batons.
13. pass out candy.
14. carry flags.
15. ride unicycles.
16. wear fancy saddles.
17. rides in a convertible.
18. sell lemonade.

**Page Twenty-seven**

| | |
|---|---|
| 1. drove | 6. cried |
| 2. flies | 7. spin |
| 3. eats | 8. galloped |
| 4. grew | 9. cheers |
| 5. splashed | |

**Page Twenty-eight**

1. ate
2. spins
3. read
4. flew
5. fly
6. sang
7. jumped
8. play
9. kicked
10. stretches
11. jumped, skipped
12. eat, run
13. danced, sparkled
14. churned, growled
15. hit, ran
16. swims, dives

**Page Twenty-nine**

| | |
|---|---|
| 1. he | 8. her |
| 2. it | 9. it |
| 3. she | 10. it |
| 4. her | 11. we |
| 5. they | 12. them |
| 6. his | 13. us |
| 7. him | |

**Page Thirty**

| | |
|---|---|
| 1. I | 6. She |
| 2. we | 7. me |
| 3. him | 8. he |
| 4. They | 9. her |
| 5. us | 10. them |

Paragraph—I, We, us, She, me, They

**Page Thirty-one**

1–12: Answers will vary.

13. warm, humid, summer
14. cool
15. private, tall
16. large
17. old, rickety
18. cool
19. Two
20. green, blue
21. new
22. hot, funny

**Page Thirty-two**

| | *Circled* | *Underlined* |
|---|---|---|
| 1. | ferocious | bear |
| 2. | chilly | room |
| 3. | powerful | wind |
| 4. | intelligent | girl |
| 5. | delicious | strawberries |
| 6. | colorful | fish |
| 7. | small | cats |
| 8. | silk | jackets |

**Page Thirty-three**

Sentences 1, 2, 3, and 7 use commas correctly.

9. Mother needs to buy lettuce, carrots, cucumbers, and mushrooms.
10. The monkey, snake, and butterfly live in the jungle.
11. The book report is due on April 14, 1997.
12. A triathlete must swim, bike, and run.
13. Maria had a dentist appointment on December 5, 1996.
14. My grandfather was born on March 23, 1940.
15. Halina likes to read, jump rope, swing, and play chess.

**Page Thirty-four**

1. Where are you going?
2. I am going mountain climbing.
3. Do you like to climb mountains?
4. Yes, I enjoy the challeng of climbing mountains.
5. Would you like to go mountain climbing with me?
6. Wow, that would be gre
7. Remember to bring a canteen of water.
8. Hurrah, I am going to climb a mountain!

**Page Thirty-five**

Sentences will vary.

**Page Thirty-six**

Sentences will vary.

**Page Forty-one**

In the first paragraph, the following words should be circled —see, pacific, Oshun, ate, it. They should be spelle as follows—sea, Pacific, Ocean, eight, It.

In the second paragraph, th following items should be circled —an, sea, of, their, ? They should be replaced as follows—An, see, off, there, .

**Page Forty-two**

February 15, 199

Dear Mr. Smith,

We are in need of new playground equipment. Ours i old and broken. The chains o the swings are broken. The slide has a crack. There are no rims on the basketball backboards, and the middle monkey bar is bent. The sandbox is empty, and all the foursquare balls have holes. We promise to take care of our new equipment.

Sincerely,
The Students

**Page Forty-five**

Activities should be completed as directed.

# Answers continued

**age Forty-six**
tivities should be completed directed.

**age Forty-seven**
. page 18
. Cats Come in All Sizes
. page 105
. Wild Elephants on Two Continents
. Birds in the Wild and in People's Homes
. Page 104

**age Forty-eight**
1. true 6. false
2. true 7. can't tell
3. true 8. true
4. false 9. can't tell
5. true

**age Forty-nine**
1. produce 6. chat
2. snooze 7. confer
3. haul 8. form
4. disguise 9. conceal
5. plodding

**age Fifty**
entences will vary.

**age Fifty-one**

| *List 1* | *List 2* |
|---|---|
| needles | seal |
| neon | skunk |
| notch | soap |
| number | stingray |
| nurse | strawberry |
| oath | taxi |
| observe | television |
| octopus | thread |
| only | tiger |
| owl | torch |

First and last words in each list should be circled.

**Page Fifty-two**
Words in these lists may appear in any order.

| *List 1* | *List 2* |
|---|---|
| anteater | hummingbird |
| beaver | jaguar |
| cheetah | llama |
| cow | lynx |
| dolphin | ostrich |
| eagle | parrot |
| fox | platypus |
| gibbon | yak |

**Page Fifty-three**
1. geyser; 8
2. spider; 18
3. nova; 14
4. telephone; 19
5. agouti; 1
6. tree; 19
7. Velcro; 20
8. colors; 4
9. Ecuador; 6
10. China; 3
11. glass; 8
12. quetzal; 16

**Page Fifty-four**
1. Livingstone, David; 12
2. Tubman, Harriet; 19
3. Colman, Bessie; 4
4. Einstein, Albert; 6
5. Monet, Claude; 13
6. Rivera, Diego; 16
7. Curie, Marie; 4
8. Winnemucca, Sarah; 21

**Page Fifty-five**
1. Canberra
2. Sydney
3. Southern Hemisphere between Indian and South Pacific Oceans
4. grassy farmlands, mountains, dry sandy desert
5. December, January, February
6. June, July, August
7. kangaroos, koalas, wallabies, wombats, platypuses
8. eucalyptus, wattle trees

**Page Fifty-six**
860 912 802 596 752
961 953 846 861 932
667 582 905 462 665
731 852 903 892 952
920 423 716 944 941
614 651 842

**Page Fifty-seven**
386 873 851 381 564
945 829 723 382 805
945 578 605 561 412
973 708 980 822 365
592 784 907 683 468
851 780 911 438 685

**Page Fifty-eight**
68 189 263 559 139
59 472 163 486 378
215 508 328 479 189
256 176 144 438
389 387 409 199

**Page Fifty-nine**
369 151 158 167
265 267 149 388
629 258 306 291
1. 25 2. 24

**Page Sixty**
Answers for each box go from left to right.
Top left box—0, 0, 0, 0, 0, 0, 0, 0, 0, 0
Middle left box—16, 12, 6, 18, 10, 14, 0, 8, 2, 4
Bottom left box—14, 9, 12, 0, 8, 4, 0, 3
Top right box—4, 9, 2, 1, 8, 6, 5, 7, 3, 0
Bottom right box—0, 15, 18, 27, 6, 21, 24, 3, 9, 12

**Page Sixty-one**
0, 0, 12, 9
18, 10, 8, 6
8, 0, 7, 24
1, 0, 27, 14
27, 10, 18, 0, 18, 6, 5
21, 4, 0, 9
16, 3, 0, 0, 0
3, 4, 0, 24, 14

**Page Sixty-two**
Riddle answer—IT CLIMBS ONTO A LEAF AND WAITS TILL FALL.

**Page Sixty-three**
12, 45, 25, 24, 0, 8, 30, 16
0, 35, 5, 36, 4, 10, 28, 40
32, 0, 15, 8, 20, 24, 20, 30
12, 45, 20, 30, 0, 10, 40, 16
15, 40, 32, 4, 0, 20, 28, 35
15, 36, 25, 24, 40, 28, 36, 10
20, 30, 28, 25, 16, 8, 40, 35
32, 16, 25, 24, 15, 4, 0, 12

**Page Sixty-four**
The problems with answers shown here in **bold print** should be circled.
**30**, 28, 18, **35**, **14**, 6, **63**, 48
42, **48**, 7, **12**, **54**, 49, 14, **18**
24, **28**, 21, **42**, 36, **56**, 6, **7**
**14**, 12, 42, **56**, **63**, 54, 35, **48**
**30**, 21, **49**, 0, **36**, 0, 24, **42**

**Page Sixty-five**
0 49 36 0
7 30 49 54
12 21 18 14
7 54 42 6
24 28 48 63
56 0 35 42
35 24 63 36
12 28 18 30
56 14 6 48
42 0 42 21
0 12
54 36

**Page Sixty-six**
48, 0, 64, 54
32, 45, 16, 72, 9, 27
72, 0, 63, 18, 56, 18
40, 81, 24, 54, 36, 40
56, 8, 45, 0, 48, 81
16, 63, 36, 64, 32, 27

**Page Sixty-seven**
81 48 18 8
72 36 32 54
0 64 27 40
56 81 16 72
63 0 9 24
45 48 18 8
72 36 32 54
56 27 40 63
24 9 64 72
9 45 16 0
63 36 64 27
72 16 45 9
81 48 18 0
54 56
32 72
72 40

**Page Sixty-eight**
2 2
5 4
5 1 6 3
1 9 8 4
3 4 7 4
6 0 9 7
3 9 8 0
1 6 5 5
7 3 7 8
2 2 9 1
0 3 8 4
5 2 5 6
3 9 3 4

# Answers continued

### Page Sixty-nine

| | | | | |
|---|---|---|---|---|
| 2 | 2 | 8 | 1 | 7 |
| 5 | 3 | 5 | 7 | 3 |
| 6 | 1 | 4 | 8 | 9 |
| 1 | 2 | 6 | 3 | 9 |
| 0 | 4 | 0 | 8 | 4 |
| 5 | 4 | 3 | 1 | |
| 3 | 4 | 6 | 6 | |
| 9 | 2 | 7 | 1 | |
| 5 | 8 | 2 | 4 | |
| 9 | 8 | | | |
| 7 | 8 | | | |
| 9 | 2 | | | |

### Page Seventy

| | | | | |
|---|---|---|---|---|
| 7 | 2 | 4 | | |
| 3 | 5 | 9 | | |
| 6 | 8 | 3 | | |
| 1 | 9 | 4 | 2 | 9 |
| 6 | 1 | 4 | 8 | 1 |
| 7 | 8 | 9 | 5 | 3 |
| 7 | 3 | 7 | 5 | 9 |
| 1 | 8 | 7 | 2 | |
| 6 | 2 | 5 | 3 | |
| 6 | 4 | 9 | 7 | |
| 8 | 4 | 4 | 2 | |
| 7 | 6 | 9 | 5 | |

### Page Seventy-one

| | | | |
|---|---|---|---|
| 6 | 5 | 5 | 6 |
| 3 | 1 | 1 | 2 |
| 9 | 4 | 8 | 9 |
| 4 | 8 | 2 | 3 |

| | | | |
|---|---|---|---|
| 7 | 9 | 2 | 1 |
| 9 | 2 | 8 | 4 |
| 4 | 5 | 6 | 3 |
| 1 | 7 | 3 | 5 |

| | | |
|---|---|---|
| 9 | 8 | 8 |
| 1 | 6 | 5 |
| 4 | 2 | 3 |
| 7 | 3 | 1 |

### Page Seventy-two

| | | | |
|---|---|---|---|
| 2 | 3 | 6 | 7 |
| 5 | 4 | 4 | 6 |
| 8 | 9 | 8 | 9 |
| 5 | 3 | 2 | 6 |
| 1 | 4 | 1 | 3 |
| 9 | 5 | 9 | 7 |
| 3 | 1 | 5 | 4 |
| 6 | 4 | 1 | 2 |

| | | | | |
|---|---|---|---|---|
| 6 | 7 | 8 | 9 | 8 |
| 7 | 0 | 8 | 3 | 2 |
| 5 | 1 | 6 | 2 | 3 |

### Page Seventy-three

A. 9 B. 2
C. 2 D. 9
E. 6 F. 4

### Page Seventy-four

| | | | |
|---|---|---|---|
| 9 | 7 | | |
| 6 | 8 | | |
| 6 | 8 | 5 | 7 |
| 3 | 9 | 1 | 4 |
| 9 | 5 | 2 | 4 |
| 1 | 3 | 2 | 8 |
| 7 | 7 | 4 | 9 |
| 4 | 2 | 5 | 9 |
| 5 | 6 | 6 | 3 |
| 1 | 3 | 9 | 5 |
| 1 | 2 | 5 | 8 |
| 4 | 2 | 8 | 6 |
| 6 | 3 | 7 | 5 |

### Page Seventy-five

| | | | | |
|---|---|---|---|---|
| 6 | 4 | 8 | 5 | 2 |
| 8 | 3 | 9 | 7 | 7 |
| 4 | 6 | 1 | 5 | 2 |
| 3 | 9 | 7 | 7 | 1 |

A. 9
B. 7
C. 8

### Page Seventy-six

1. No; The paragraph does not give names of flowers.
2. Yes; The rainbow lorikeet is many different colors.
3. No; It does not say where the packs sleep.

### Page Seventy-eight

1. elephant
2. cheetah
3. lizard
4. porcupine
5. raccoon
6. turtle
7. penguin
8. blue whale

### Page Seventy-nine

1. hard
2. cold
3. huge
4. bee
5. sour
6. light
7. old
8. floating
9. bottom
10. bird
11. cake
12. envelope
13. tree

### Page Eighty

A. first kitten—white with orange yarn; second kitten—striped with light blue yarn; third kitten—spotted with dark blue yarn; fourth kitten—brown with green yarn

B. Tom, Quentin, Pat, Rosa, Sue

### Page Eighty-one

Problem A

Row 1—hexagon, parallelogram, star, oval
Row 2—parallelogram, star, oval, hexagon
Row 3—star, oval, hexagon, parallelogram
Row 4—oval, hexagon, parallelogram, star

Problem B

Row 1—green, green, red, green, green, red
Row 2—yellow, blue, yellow, blue, yellow, blue
Row 3—blue, red, blue, red, blue, red
Row 4—yellow, green, green, yellow, green, green
Row 5—red, blue, yellow, red, blue, yellow

### Page Eighty-two

A. Sue—triangle
Bob—oval
Nick—square
Jean—circle

B. first—Alonzo
second—Alanna
third—Bill
fourth—Carla
fifth—Hector

C. Mia—blue, green, red
Ted—green, yellow
Cathie—green, red

### Page Eighty-three

Accept reasonable answers.

### Page Eighty-four

Accept reasonable answers.

### Page Eighty-five

| | | | |
|---|---|---|---|
| G6 | snake | B3 | bear |
| A5 | lion | D6 | sheep |
| H2 | tiger | H5 | camel |
| E4 | bird | F1 | giraffe |

### Page Eighty-six

| | | | |
|---|---|---|---|
| B1 | A7 | C8 | A4 |
| D2 | C5 | E6 | H1 |
| H4 | G8 | F3 | G6 |

### Page Eighty-seven

Symbols should be drawn on map as directed.

### Page Eighty-eight

1. Bear Branch Village
2. North
3. Brown Bear Village
4. Grizzly Town
5. Bear Junction
6. South
7. East
8. West

### Page Eighty-nine

1. Jake
2. Mitzi
3. 3
4. Sami
5. Sue and Jess
6. 7
7. 7
8. 3
9. Mary, Jake, and Sami

### Page Ninety

1. 14 boxes
2. 3
3. apples
4. 20
5. tangerines
6. 5
7. 9
8. bananas and peaches
9. nectarines and oranges

### Page Ninety-one

1. March
2. 1
3. September
4. 53
5. January
6. 1
7. 9
8. August

### Page Ninety-two

1. Joe and Lynne
2. Colin
3. Dave
4. Tracy and Colin
5. Kristin
6. Week 3
7. Week 2